SO-AXJ-569

DATE DUE

OCT 0 6

FAILURE

FAILURE

AN AUTOBIOGRAPHY

❧

Joshua Gidding

Plainville Public Library
56 East Main Street
Plainville, CT 06062

CYAN

Copyright © 2007 Joshua Gidding

First published in 2007 by:

Cyan Communications Limited
30 Bond Street
New York, NY 10012
United States of America
T: +1 (718) 701 1217
E: sales@cyanbooks.com

and

Cyan Communications Limited
119 Wardour Street
London W1F 0UW
United Kingdom
T: +44 (0)20 7565 6120
E: sales@cyanbooks.com

www.cyanbooks.com

The right of Joshua Gidding to be identified as the author of this work has
been asserted by him in accordance with the Copyright, Designs and Patents
Act 1988.

All rights reserved

The author is grateful to Apple Corp./Capitol Records for permission to quote
from The Beatles' "Nowhere Man", and to Special Rider Music for permission
to quote from Bob Dylan's "Love Minus Zero/No Limit". Extract from "My
Whole Life", translated by W.S. Merwin, from *Selected Poems* by Jorge Luis
Borges, edited by Alexandra Coleman, copyright © 1999 by Maria Kodama;
used by permission of Viking Penguin, a division of Penguin Group (USA) Inc.

All reasonable efforts have been made to obtain necessary copyright permissions
for quoted extracts. Any copyright omissions or errors are unintentional and
will, if notified to the publisher, be rectified in any future printings.

No part of this publication may be reproduced, stored in a retrieval system or
transmitted in any form or by any means including photocopying, electronic,
mechanical, recording or otherwise, without the prior written permission of
the rights holders, application for which must be made to the publisher.

A CIP record for this book is available from the British Library

ISBN-13 978-1-905736-21-8
ISBN-10 1-905736-21-5

Printed and bound in Great Britain by
TJ International Ltd, Padstow, Cornwall

3 2535 11052 5174

For Diane
always and forever

Contents

Acknowledgments

Greg, Sue and David Todd introduced me to Catherine Aman, who put me in touch with my editor, Stephanie Staal, who, together with Martin Liu, had the courage to take this book on. Kilty Gilmour was the first to read the manuscript, and her encouragement meant very much to me. Dowling College gave me the released time and sabbatical leave that enabled me to write it.

I thank all of them, and am deeply grateful.

"There's no success like failure,
and failure's no success at all."

Bob Dylan, "Love Minus Zero/No Limit"

1

The Territory of Failure

Who am I, that I should presume to write my autobiography?

I am not famous, or notorious, or in any way distinguished.

I am, in fact, a nobody. A failure. First and foremost, a failed novelist. (See Chapter 8.) My only published novel came out over 25 years ago, to no acclaim, and mixed reviews. *People Magazine* panned it, called its insights "forgettable." As it turned out, they were prescient. Here I am, 25 years and several more unpublishable novels later, my early promise unfulfilled, and now forgotten. And with good reason: there was no follow-up. (Lack of follow-up is one of my failures.)

In that first novel, I chose some lines from a poem by Borges for my epigraph:

I believe that my days and my nights, in
their poverty and their riches, are the
equal of God's and of all men's.

I admit I still believe this; only now I hold that belief in the ironic light, rather than under the triumphant banner, of youthful great expectations. How I love that phrase, "great expectations!" And not ironically, either; for it is the marching song of youth—the remembered marching song of youth, mine included. Which is not to say that I do not still nourish great expectations, of a sort—or at least good ones. But now they are the modified expectations of middle-aged retrenchment, nourished in the light—the antique light, muted, nostalgic—of the awareness of failure.

You might say this book is a study—a case study, written by the case himself—in the awareness, the sensibility, of failure. If I were a real scholar—that is, if I were a successful or serious scholar, rather than an intellectual dilettante—I might even undertake a cultural/historical study of failure, à la Foucault. Such a project (I can see it now, in all its ambitious glory, shining with great expectations!) would be groundbreaking, important, original. In the words of my imagined future reviewers, perhaps even "magisterial." (I am rather fond of that word too, peering at me smugly over its scholar's half-glasses.) To have gotten to the point of writing a "magisterial study" seems an achievement of no small note. Such a study, were it to be published, might even be career-making, serving to propel me into greener pastures, fairer courts of academic life. But I will not write such a study. It is beyond me. (See Chapter 10.) I will content myself with an autobiographical account of failure as I have come to know it.

I am well qualified to write such a book. But does a failed writer even have the right to call himself a writer? I say yes. After all, it's not as if I'm boasting, or laying claim to a sought-after status, or pretending to be something I'm not. At this point, this more-than-midpoint in my life (I am over 50), I have been a failed writer for over 25 years.

Perhaps you detect a paradox here. For if you are reading this book, that must mean it was published. And if it was published, that must mean it is not a failure. (At least not a complete failure.)

And if it is not really a failure, then I cannot claim to be a failed writer. True enough. But remember, since I am in the process of writing this, it isn't yet completed, let alone published. It may never be completed—let alone published. And so, as of this writing, any paradox that you detect along those lines is based on assumptions about completion and publication that have yet to be fulfilled. Besides, what's wrong with paradoxes? We can live with paradoxes. This attempted book of mine, unlike any other attempted (or perpetrated) book of mine, may not prove to be a failure in the end. That would be ironic, wouldn't it? It would be an irony I could live with. Yet would it not also be, this failure of my book to fail, something of a disappointment? Perhaps. Insofar as there is that in me which seeks failure, rather than success, I admit it would probably be a disappointment. But a disappointment I could live with. It would certainly be different from living with, and nurturing, as I have for so long, the curiously buoying self-satisfactions, self-justifications, and self-vindications of failure, whose pleasures are so akin to the luxurious self-pity of childhood injuries and illnesses. But I could live with it. And if not—if this book, like all the others, should turn out a failure in the end? Well then, there would be poetic justice in that outcome: for how could a book entitled *Failure* have failed to be otherwise?

But whatever the outcome proves to be doesn't really concern me. What concerns me is the journey. The journey into the territory of failure.

The territory of failure is virgin land: if not exactly undiscovered, then unexplored, at least in the way that I propose to explore it. The territory of failure is a part of our country that remains off the map, for one reason or another. One of the reasons may be because it is depressing, because (supposedly) no one wants to hear about failure. But this isn't really true. We secretly like hearing about other people's failures. Especially the failures of the rich and famous—the excessively rich and undeservedly famous (of which there seems to be an increasing number).

In the failures of others we find our own failures diminished, perhaps even vindicated, turned into signs of our underlying virtue, which was there all along, despite the doubts of others, and even ourselves. If nothing else, we find a certain self-exculpatory relief in the recognition of the failures of others: At least we didn't do *that*; at least we don't have ourselves to blame for *that*. (This is the exact reverse of the "grass is always greener" syndrome.)

Another reason for the neglect of failure in American culture may be because the exploration of failure, and the dwelling on it (if not the wallowing in it!), doesn't accord well with our national narrative of success. And not just a narrative: an obsession. We are obsessed with success, and terrified of failure. Always have been. Even when we are relieved by the failure of others, we are still terrified by it. In fact, the relief is probably just a cover for the terror, because we know that their failure could also be ours.

Well, I am here to tell you that you don't have to be afraid anymore. You can sit back and enjoy it—not only others' failure, but your own. It's OK. Failure is good for you. In fact, it's better for you than success, in some ways.

Of course this is well known, and always has been. There is a spiritual content in failure that is utterly lacking in success. Any loser knows this. We feel purified and ennobled, in a way, by our defeats, as we never do in victory. The Bible tells us it is better to go to the house of mourning than to the house of mirth. While I wouldn't go that far—I am too fond of the house of mirth—I will say that I am also rather fond of the house of mourning. The house of mourning is a place to which I have become very attached. I have been living in the house of mourning for almost three years now, since my wife died. I find it familiar and comforting. It was, after all, her house too. No, I am not at all averse to the house of mourning. But you don't need to join me there. All I'm asking you to consider is that the wilderness of failure is a more inspiring place than the cultivated (overcultivated, as far as I'm concerned) fields of success. It is also a more interesting place, for a number of reasons.

"Speaking of spiritual matters—you are the voice of despair," you object. "You counsel despair. Yours is the counsel of despair."

Not at all. I am more of a *vox clamantis in deserto*. The *deserto* just happens to be the wilderness of failure. And, like all deserts, it is a place of beauty, and of unexpected life, too. You just have to know where to look. Is it presumptuous, even insane, to suggest that, not entirely unlike that earlier *vox,* I too am a harbinger of hope—the hope that lies in failure?

"Yes," you reply. "It is presumptuous. Very presumptuous. And also insane. But putting that aside for the moment, it is not just failure you are counseling; it is the cultivation of failure as well. It is the cultivation of failure that you would have us take up in your desert. You mention the 'cultivated fields of success,' but you are asking us to cultivate failure. Not only is this insane, it is also unnatural, even inhuman. What you are counseling is, finally, something inhuman. Which is the most important reason why it must be rejected."

Yes, you are right—to counsel failure would be both unnatural and inhuman, I agree. But that's not really what I'm doing. I am not counseling failure, I am observing it, analyzing it, talking about it, based on my own experience—and in doing so, encouraging others to talk about it, too. Because our failures are among the things we don't like to talk about. We have our reasons for not liking to talk about them. They are good reasons, even: Failure is upsetting, it is unpleasant, it is depressing; the very idea, or remembrance, of our failure makes us uncomfortable, anxious, afraid, and ashamed. But precisely for that reason, reader, precisely for that very reason, failure must be confronted, it must be taken up, it must be told—however great the shame.

For failure is America's dirty little secret. Even in our therapeutic culture, failure is something we cannot forgive ourselves.

And so we do not talk of it at all. We hide it, we bury it, we try to forget it. But it is my job, my self-appointed, gratuitious, yet necessary job to dig it up and expose it to the light of day.

Or, to use another metaphor: We are all familiar with the old saw that good medicine does not taste good. Quite the opposite: good medicine usually tastes bad. There is even recognized to be, in the conventional wisdom at least, a direct relationship between the badness of the medicine's taste and the goodness of its action. And so it may be with this inquiry; this inquiry may be a kind of medicine, too. A medicine as yet untried in our therapeutic culture. I take my cue from Kierkegaard:

> …Then one Sunday afternoon, four years ago, I was sitting out in a café in the Fredericksberg Garden smoking my cigar and looking at the servant-girls and suddenly the idea struck me: you go on wasting your time without profit; on every side one genius after another appears and makes life and existence, and the historical means of conveyance and communication with eternal happiness, easier and easier—what do you do? Could you not discover some way in which you too could help the age? Then I thought, what if I sat down and made everything difficult? … For if no one is prepared to make it difficult it becomes all too easy … .

What Kierkegaard proposed to do for difficulty, I propose, in my own minor way, to do for failure.

2

The Failure of My Childhood

How is this possible? What exactly does it mean, the "failure" of a childhood? How could someone actually have a "failed childhood"? Because they were forced to work in a blacking factory, or a cotton plantation? Certainly, that would be one example; but then we really shouldn't speak of the "failure" of their childhood (for that would imply some culpability on their part), but rather the "stealing" of their childhood from them. But we're not going there. This isn't a political or historical book. (Come to think of it, another of my failures is the failure to be politically or historically engaged.)

My childhood can be considered a "failed" one in that I failed to have an "authentic childhood," because of where, and how, I grew up—in the lap of luxury, in Pacific Palisades, California. To have grown up thus is to have had a failed childhood. I know that many will disagree with this, both those who grew up in the Palisades and privileged places like it, and those who didn't. They may be right. After all, children—rich as well as poor—are not to blame for where and how they grow up. They cannot be blamed for being sent to the blacking factory, or the cotton plantation—and they cannot be blamed for being sent to riding lessons, either. (Unless it was their idea, and they begged their parents for the riding lessons, and maybe a horse to go along with the lessons, and their parents consented. Then they can be blamed, the whole rich, spoiled-rotten bunch of them can be blamed.)

But even though the riding lessons were not my idea, and I cannot be blamed, I still feel guilty, and tainted with the failure of inauthenticity. Because I, too, was a child of privilege, who got my riding lessons in third grade. But no horse. I never wanted one. I was afraid of them. Afraid, and uneasy. Afraid of their hooves, of being kicked in the skull by those powerful hooves, attached to those powerful legs. And uneasy because I felt guilty for burdening their backs, their strong, hot, sweaty, exploited and enslaved backs with my weight, light as it was in third grade. I worried sometimes that I would break their backs.

My riding teacher was Frank. He was English. He had a cockney accent—or so my mother said. She was in a position to know, because we had just spent nearly a year living in London, first at the Dorchester Hotel, then in a two-story flat in Mayfair. Cambridge-educated tutor for me, then a private day school, where the burden of privilege was almost made up for by having to wear short pants in winter (outdoor soccer games in Hyde Park an agony), a sadistic math ("maths") teacher, and disgusting food that I was forced to eat. (I remember in particular the greasy, leaden dumplings, the waterlogged "greens," and the steak-and-kidney pie, with urinous kidneys.) Yes, I had my share of privileged misery at St. David's, which I suppose was good from the point of view of a failed childhood, inasmuch as misery suffered and survived can be considered authenticating. And so, when we returned home to the Palisades after almost a year in London, my mother wanted me to have riding lessons as a way of continuing my "English experience." Not because she was a snob—she was proud, in her gently rueful way, of having been born middle-class and Irish Catholic in Scranton, PA—but because she was a sentimentalist, an empath, and a romantic, and did not want the romance (to her, who had not had to eat the urinous kidneys) of my nine months in England to be totally lost. She thought that riding lessons with Frank, the cockney riding teacher, were a way of keeping the faith, in a way that was socially acceptable to one of her egalitarian values.

Frank was a short, trim, bronzed man, neatly groomed, with a weather-beaten face. He taught me to post, then canter—all within the confines of the small outdoor corral at Kenter Stables, at the rustic end of Kenter Avenue, in the hills of Brentwood. A cockney in the Santa Monica Mountains—as we had been Southern Californians in London. That was the bond I felt (or my mother felt) I had with him—that, and the fact that I was not one of the snooty rich girls who kept their horses at the stables, and who gave Frank a hard time when their "Valentine" or their "Rebel" had missed a grooming, or an exercising, or a reshoeing, or whatever it was they reminded him they were paying him for. Maybe I also identified Frank with the ostler in the poem "The Highwayman," by Alfred Noyes, which I'd had to memorize the beginning of at St. David's ("The moon was a ghostly galleon, tossed upon cloudy seas"/something, something/"The road was a ribbon of moonlight, over the purple moor/And the highwayman came riding, riding, riding/The highwayman came riding, up to the old inn door.") Or maybe it was my mother who had that idea, too; it probably was.

It certainly was my mother who first took an intense dislike to the snooty horse-girls, and their mistreatment of Frank; and it became a source of pride with me, instilled and nourished by her, that I was not one of them. Pride, and a certain self-congratulation. The two are so close. The welling in the breast that is the feeling of honest pride can so easily slide into the defensive preening of self-congratulation. Or so it has often been with me.

My thinking went something like this: "I may be a child of privilege, not unlike those snooty horse-girls (or even, 'I may be seen by Frank as a child of privilege too, coming to my riding lessons in my private-school uniform'), but at least I'm not actually *one* of the snooty horse-girls, and I never will be, not as long as I live, and no matter what I do." Filtered through my mother's hyper-responsive sensibilities, the guilt I felt at the perceived disparity between my lot and Frank's, and his possible perception of it too, were translated instantly into the throb of a compensatory and gratuitous self-congratulation.

"So isn't it really guilt, and not failure, you're talking about?" you ask. "Isn't it really the sense of guilt over unearned privilege, and not really the sense of failure at all, that besets you?" Your point is well-taken, but will not keep me from my appointed rounds. There is room enough in this journey for guilt—there is certainly room enough! Guilt and failure, you see, are two peas in a pod; and the exploratory approach I take toward failure is taken also toward guilt. They are intimately related. They are kindred spirits. Failure, in American culture, produces guilt, by way of blame and self-blame. And does it also work the other way? Does guilt also produce failure? How could it not? You (I mean, I) carry around this load of guilt, and you're bound to fail at something sooner or later. (In my case, sooner.) And then the guilt, and the failure, begin to compound. Ah, the riches of compound interest, guilt and failure, compounded daily! Yes, they are inevitably tied together. And so do not worry, reader, and be of good cheer: Guilt will be our ever-present companion in this journey, this long day's journey into failure.

The feeling of things being "too easy," of there being a lack of difficulty in my life, was something I had often as a child. I see it now as another aspect of the sense of a failed childhood, of having somehow missed out on having an authentic childhood. But back then, in my childhood itself, the sense of things being "too easy" occurred as a feeling in my balls. A feeling of lightness in my balls—an uneasy feeling. An uneasy feeling of things just being "too easy." This feeling was not unlike the effect produced in my balls of temporary weightlessness when on a carnival ride such as the Tilt-a-Whirl. It was a curious feeling, and bears further attention.

I got this same feeling when I would think about people suffering, while being conscious, at the same time, that I myself was not suffering. That I was fortunate and privileged, and that there was, simultaneously in some other place in the world—India, let's say—a person, and more to the point, a child, who was suffering. Who was hungry, perhaps starving to death, or blind, crippled, or horribly sick—even unto death. (These were not all the same child. Even I wouldn't have gone that far.) The awareness of the contrast between our two different lots in life was what would produce a sort of sympathetic vibration down in my balls. The feeling in the balls acted as a kind of visceral register of the image of suffering. I should add that the feeling was not entirely unpleasant. I was aware of this even at the time. And this awareness brought its own little accompaniment of guilt. (I'm not going to try to figure that one out; I'll leave that one to you, reader. The ball—the balls—are in your court.)

The reference to India just now was not gratuitous. For three months in 1961–62, before moving to London, we lived in India. From Bonner School, and Mrs. Gray's second-grade classroom, where we had just learned to sing "America" and "America the Beautiful," to New Delhi and the Imperial Hotel, and then a house in an exclusive colony, with servants. Many servants, including: a cook, Ali; a "bearer" (combination butler and waiter), Baksh; an "aya" (nanny), Rosie (a Christian, from Goa); a "chokidar" (night-watchman); a gardener; a driver; a launderer; and a "sweeper" (the Untouchable, Natu; more of him anon). This was quite a change for a seven-year-old. True, it was a trans-plantation from one bastion of privilege to another: from home in the Palisades and private school in Brentwood to the Imperial

Hotel (I doubt it is still called that) in New Delhi, and then the Haz Kaz Colony and the International School. But, I being the son of a Catholic-educated empath from Scranton, PA, you can be sure I was not allowed to remain completely insulated in my privileged bubble. Carpooling to and from the International School through the streets of New Delhi; going out with my parents to dinner in Old Delhi; trips to the Taj Mahal, Bombay, and Kathmandu.

What made the greatest impression during these excursions, however, was not the splendors of man and nature, but the unimaginable poverty, filth, suffering, and disease.

More than anything, the beggars. Old men and young men and women and children, my age and younger, following us on the street, running after us in our car or taxi, coming up to the window when we stopped at a light. My mother, I see now, was in something of a double bind due to her dual role as my protector and my moral instructor—not to mention her own nature as an empath. As my protector, she wanted to do her best to shield me from the violent spectacle of suffering on such a grand scale, as well as keep from me God only knows what diseases that might slip past the cordon of our immunizations. But as my moral instructor, she could not shield me too much from the necessary reality of suffering. And as an empath herself, she could not run away—not always, anyway—from people in need. When to give, and how much? And when, and how, to stop giving? Impossible lessons to learn; inevitable failures of adequate response in the face of infinite need. The children everywhere, running after us, swarming around us on the street; the blind and the lame, sitting, lying in the street. It was overwhelming, confusing, shaming, and guilt-begetting. Who was I, to have been born in wealth and health and plenty? Who were they, to have been born in poverty and misery and disease? What was my obligation, and where did it end? No doubt those three months in India were formative chapters in the story of my sense of failure, the development of my guilt, the growth of my capacity and hunger for suffering.

The Great Triumverate of my childhood, the guardian spirits and tutelary gods of my conscience: failure, guilt, and suffering. Without those three months in India, I doubt I would have become the devotee that I am.

It was also the "Indian experience," as my mother would say, that was behind the strange response I sometimes had to music as a child. This response was a variation on the uneasy, light feeling in the balls—or rather an intensification of it, exacerbated by the felt indifference of the happy music to the imagined suffering of children (especially Indian children). It was the perceived celebratory, sensual elements in the music—elements that I now see I responded strongly to, in spite of myself (that is, in spite of my suffering self)—that I then saw as at odds with my awareness of suffering in the world. Here I was, bopping to the beat of "Thank You, Girl," or "She's a Woman," or "Twist and Shout," really loving it—at least really loving it in my chest and my ears, as it were. While in my stomach and balls there was the uneasy feeling, brought on by the images in my mind's eye—both in imagination and memory—of the Indian children, with flies swarming around their eyes. The music was playing and my heart was throbbing with excitement, while the suffering children were fixed tenaciously in my inner eye. Sometimes they were speaking, too—begging me for money, which I would give, but it didn't matter. It was like a movie in my mind that I wanted to turn off but couldn't. Not until the music stopped. At which point the images would subside, as though they were merely an inflamed response to the irritant that was the music, and the happiness and excitement that accompanied it. It was as if I had to pay for the happiness I felt with the images of suffering that went with it.

During the year we were living in India and England, a man was living in our house back in the Palisades and taking care of it. His name was Paul Kirschner. He was from Solingen, Germany—the world capital of "precision instruments," as he liked to say. He'd come to America around the time of World War I, to avoid serving in the Kaiser's army, and fighting in the Kaiser's war. This would have made him about 65 years old in 1961–62. No spring chicken, but not quite ready to retire yet. Besides, he loved my father. He'd first started working for us a few years before, when my father got a flat tire and Paul, who happened to be driving by at the time, stopped and helped him change it. It turned out that Paul was very handy, and my father (who wasn't at all) was in need of such a person. So Paul began doing odd jobs around the house and garden, sometimes babysitting for me as well. He was divorced, and his daughter Gundel, who I remember as very beautiful, lived with her mother in Brentwood, in an apartment that Paul managed. He stayed at the house for the year we were away, and when we returned, Paul moved into my room.

Friends I've told about this think it's weird that I had an old German man sleeping in my room for three years, and I suppose it was. But it must have been just as weird for Paul, being of retirement age and having to sleep in the same room as an eight-year-old kid who wet his bed every night, and was prone to self-inflicted constipation. (I considered subtitling this section "The Failure of My Toilet-Training.") I don't imagine Paul was terribly fond of having to change my urine-soaked sheets on those mornings when my mother just wasn't up to the task. Nor could he have enjoyed the brief misadventure of the electric sheet. This was a urine-sensitive device that went under my bottom sheet, and was connected by wires to a box that sounded an alarm as soon as the nocturnal stream began to issue from my ungovernable penis. The idea behind the "electric sheet" was a Pavlovian one: After being woken up in the middle of the night a few times by the shrieking alarm, my lax bladder was supposed to learn to control itself.

But it didn't quite work out that way. The first night the alarm sounded, I became hysterical, and my mom and Paul had quite a job calming me down. The second night, I slept through it and soaked the electric sheet. There was no third night.

I'm sure Paul was as relieved as I was. Being startled out of bed in the middle of the night must have been especially bothersome for him, because he had an artificial leg. At night, after the lights were out, he would remove the leg and its straps and do something with them, so that I never, ever, laid eyes on it. But I knew something was going on, because of the nighttime sounds, and the way he walked, with a limp, and a creaking sound. But because I loved him, and because I was a dreamy rather than observant child, and because my parents did not try to avoid the subject so much as they just ignored it—probably a wise approach where artificial legs and young children are concerned—I did not inquire any further. I just accepted the sounds, including the dismantling and arranging in the dark, as part of the familiar presence that was Paul.

I said that I never laid eyes on the leg, but that is not quite true. I did, once. Paul was sitting in a chair in the garden, and the bottom of his trousers had hiked up a little, so that a flesh-colored bit of leg was showing. But something was not quite right about the leg—it was too flesh-colored, and it was shiny. I immediately forced myself not to look, and felt not only horrified but guilty, as though I'd been spying on him and his secret, and also terribly sorry for him, as though he were suddenly exposed in all of his vulnerability. But even though the evidence of the leg's artificiality was now incontrovertible, I still did not fully admit it to myself, as if to do so would only add insult to injury (so to speak), and constitute a further betrayal of him. So I just continued to put out of my mind the evidence of what I'd seen, and what I heard when he walked, and the mysterious sounds at night. When, a few years later, I finally did ask my mom about the leg, she said Paul had lost it in a car accident. But I wonder. Maybe that's just what he'd told her. Maybe he hadn't escaped the Kaiser's army after all, but had lost it in the war. That would make him a kind of hero—which is just fine with me.

❧

If my bed-wetting, and its abortive nonremedy, were understandably bothersome to Paul, my idiosyncratic bowel habits were not nearly as problematic for him. He possibly even liked them. That was because he had an easy solution for them (easy for him, anyway): mineral-oil enemas. Now, to understand the desperate times that called for these desperate measures, it is necessary to go back a few years, to the pre-Paul years—to the years of Eleanor Solomon, head of Hill & Dale Nursery School and Kindergarten. Eleanor Solomon had some strict ideas about toilet training, and since my mother didn't really have any ideas at all on the subject—at least not any that she was prepared to act upon; she just didn't want to deal with it at all—she basically left matters up to Eleanor Solomon. Big mistake. Eleanor Solomon was the Mr. Gradgrind of toilet training.

My problem (if it even was a problem, until Eleanor started "treating" it) was really very simple: I just didn't want to go to the bathroom in any toilet not my own. When I had to go and I wasn't at home (which meant, when I was at Hill & Dale, because where else was I going to be?), I would simply hold back my bowel movement. At these times I would get an even more dreamy, distracted, or suspiciously concentrated look on my face (and, for some weird reason, goosebumps all over my arms, sides, and scalp). My classmates were none the wiser—which was just the way I wanted them—but Eleanor had me pegged. That faraway, pensive look didn't fool her. At such times she would take me aside and whisper, rather eagerly, "Josh, do you have to go to the bathroom?" I denied it, of course. Asking a kid like me if he had to go to the bathroom was like asking him if he had shit his pants. "Yeah right, Eleanor—I shit my pants, and I want to tell you all about it." But Eleanor Solomon was not to be put off in such matters: you might say she was a harrier hound of the rectum. "I think you need to go to the bathroom, Josh." And she would take me into the dread Blue Room, with its several cubicles that, if memory serves me right, were open in the front, to permit easy surveillance by whoever wanted to look. (A kind of preschool version, it was to occur to me many years later, in grad school, of the Foucauldian "panopticon." But although she was definitely into disciplining and punishing, I doubt whether Eleanor was into Foucault.) What, kids have privacy? Not in Eleanor's bathroom. This place of horrors was virtually synonymous, for me, with impaction. And then—she would lock me in, telling me I couldn't come out until I "went." Good thinking, Eleanor. Needless to say, I didn't emerge from the Blue Room until my mom came to pick me up. With the deed left undone, of course.

Not only did such anti-toilet training create in me an inordinate attachment to the Home Toilet, which persists to this day, as well as an aversion to All Other Toilets (this, fortunately, I have outgrown—though it took boarding school to do it). It also gave me some rather confused ideas relating to my own, and other people's, fecal products. For instance, one day after a swimming lesson (it was at Hill & Dale that I learned to swim; and here the swimming instructor, "Sollie" Solomon, Eleanor's husband, was as much a *mensch* as his wife was a harridan), I spied a little turd at the bottom of the pool. Assuming it was mine (after all, I figured, with my checkered history at Hill & Dale, who else's could it be?), I dove down and retrieved it, then wrapped it in my towel, and hid with it in the bathroom, until Guess Who eventually discovered me. And it. Except it turned out not to be mine at all—as I learned the next day from my first love, Cathy Meyn, who confessed to me that she'd gone to the bathroom in the swimming pool the day before.

Now *that* was love.

Is it any surprise that by the time grade school came around, I was already an expert bowel-movement-holder-backer? (Is there a single word in German to express this idea? And did Paul know it? I'll bet he did. He certainly knew what to do about it.) If the urge came upon me at school—which it usually didn't, my bowels having adjusted themselves not only to my biological clock, but also to my twisted psychological one—I would simply hold it back, and go when I got home, the sight of my Home Toilet having about the same loosening effect on my colon as the sight of Ithaca on Odysseus's heartstrings. The real problem began in the spring of third grade, when I began to attend the Tocaloma Boys' Club on Tuesday and Thursday afternoons. The dark green bus—it looked more like an old panel truck, except longer, with room for about 12 boys—would pick me up at school, and we would go to Stoner Park (*sic*), where we would play kickball, handball ("Chinese" style), softball, touch football, basketball, or capture-the-flag. When it was very hot, we might go to the pool at the Tocaloma clubhouse on Little Santa Monica Blvd. in West L.A., right across from the Mormon Temple, with its huge statue of Joseph Smith, or whoever it was, blowing his horn on top; or, when it was raining, play games inside the clubhouse. I loved Tocaloma—not just the sports, but the Indian "tribes" you "belonged" to (Braves, Apaches, Cherokees, and Sioux, corresponding roughly to third, fourth, fifth, and sixth grades), and the system of merit badges and promotions you would work your way up to.

But it wrought havoc on my bowels for the first year or so. Because now, when the urge came, I not only had to hold back at school, but at Tocaloma as well. The public toilets at Stoner Park were strictly out of the question, and the ones at the clubhouse, while less unsightly, were also unacceptable to one as finicky as I. The result was that sometimes, on an ill-omened Tuesday or Thursday, I would hold back for the entire day, and when I got home I no longer had the urge to go at all. What I had instead was a cramp in my left side—sometimes so bad that I could hardly walk, and would have to take to my bed. At such times, my mom tried Milk of Magnesia, but either I would gag on the foul substance and not be able to swallow it, or I would manage to get it down but it would do no good. And the shame and humiliation of Ex-Lax, the stuff of juvenile ridicule, were such that it was not to be considered. Although Paul swore by it (and that certainly was no recommendation, in my book; Paul also swore by Brylcreem, Lawrence Welk, and "professional" wrestling—"Ja, just give him good once the old heart-punch, ya big palooka!"), it was a heinous travesty of chocolate, and only reminded me of the thing it was supposed to provoke.

It was time for Herr Doktor Paul. The German cure for bowel-movement-holding-back was simple and effective. No bad taste, no phony chocolate. The only thing was, it involved inserting a Vaseline-besmeared hard rubber tube into my rectum, while either Paul or my mother literally held the bag, which was filled with a mixture of warm water and mineral oil. And that was only the beginning. Moments after insertion, I would feel my stomach—or whatever it was inside of me that was being enemized—fill to bursting. It felt like my guts were going to explode. The very thought of this gruesome procedure made me nearly crazed with dread.

"No! No!" I screamed from my bed. "No enema! Please, no enema!"

"Just see once how good it's gonna work, Goshua," Paul coaxed. (For some reason he could never pronounce my name correctly.) "Try it once and you'll be feelin' like a million dollars."

"No enema!"

My mom smoothed my hair as I lay curled up on my side to ease the pain. She spoke soothingly in her empath voice in a way that went straight to my heart—but bypassed my impacted bowels.

"Joshie, sweetie, we've got to do something, honey. You won't take Milk of Magnesia, and you won't take Ex-Lax. And you'll see," and here her voice began to grow brighter and hopeful, she was seeing the light at the end of the tunnel (so to speak), as though from my point of view, "you'll see, it'll be over in a flash, and you'll feel such *relief*." Mom was big on relief—physical relief, psychological relief, maybe even spiritual relief (though as a lapsed Catholic, that one was a tougher row for her to hoe). She looked imploringly at Paul. The good doctor Paul.

"Let's try it once and you'll see now, Goshua. You'll see how it'll be smooth sailin'." This was a favorite term of his, but here the nautical metaphor was misplaced. What he had planned for me wasn't a boat trip, it was a lube job.

"No enema," I repeated. But my voice was softening, my will weakening. The chase was nearing its end. More smoothing of the hair.

"All right," coaxed Mom, "then let's try some more Milk of Magnesia."

"No."

"Ex-La—?"

"No!"

Smooth, smooth, smooth. "Come on, sweetie. It'll be over before you know it."

Well, she was half-right. It was soon over—but not before I knew it. I knew it all too well: the obscene, greased insertion; the raising of the pink bag, the color of raw veal (from when Paul made sauerbraten); the frightening bloating of the guts; then the disgusting, humiliating peeing of the mineral oil–water mixture out of the butt, just like a girl (as far as I knew, anyway). Sometimes it took a few tries to dislodge the impacted mass. And when it finally plopped out, it hurt, despite all the greasing and oiling, because it was so large and hard. It hurt so much it made me cry. But at last, it was out of me. And Mom was absolutely right about one thing: Relief was the best feeling of all. Never again.

Until the next time.

But Paul was much more than my enema-tormentor (there must be a German word for that, too). He would stay with me for weeks at a time when my parents traveled without me—which didn't happen often, but made a big impression when it did. I remember my seventh birthday, when they were away in India, where my father was researching a film on the assassination of Gandhi (*Nine Hours to Rama*), and they were making the necessary arrangements to rent a house for the three months we would be living there later that year. It was a strange birthday, lonely and foggy (June in coastal L.A. is almost always a foggy month), and the treasure trove of presents my parents had bought for me before they left—a woodburning set, a do-it-yourself "stained-glass" kit, a miniature golf course we set up on the back lawn—seemed forlorn and incomplete without them. My birthday party had been in May, before my parents left, and so for my real birthday—June 3—there were only Paul and Tracy, the girl from across the street. Tracy was limber, athletic, and pretty, and all through grade school she held me in thrall: her long dark-brown hair reaching all the way down her back, the fascinating dark girl-hair on her arms, her casual cruelty (she liked to pour salt on snails and watch them ooze green froth before they died), the way she would charm the waitresses every year on her birthday at Lawry's The Prime Rib, when she would ask for her meat "blood rare," and her insatiable appetite for Firestix. Paul had a sweet spot for her, too. He loved watching her turn cartwheels and handsprings on the back lawn. He would shake his head fondly and make a characteristic squeaking sound with his lips. "That Tracy, she's a real tomboy, all right," he said. "See now once what she doin' here. You better watch out when she get older, she gonna make all the boys go bananas."

When we were away for a year, Paul made a concrete base for the mailbox, and had Tracy put her seven-year-old handprints in the wet concrete. Years later, the base cracked, and we replaced it, but the part with Tracy's handprints was intact, so we put it in the garden. In October of 2004, long after Paul was gone, and after my mother, my father, and my wife had all died, I sold the old house on Vance Street, and had one last party the night before the new owners took possession. Tracy came to the party. Though I hadn't seen her in over 35 years, she looked much the same: slim, athletic, excited, her dark blue eyes sparkling. As she was leaving, I took her into the garden to show her the concrete slab with her seven-year-old handprints still on it. We agreed she had to take it. She picked up the slab herself and put it in the trunk of her SUV. Then she turned to me and asked, "Who was Paul?"

I gave her an answer that does not please me to remember now—and did not please me at the time, either. I was speaking for effect, I suppose, and ironically—as a self-conscious commentary on my privileged childhood, the last physical remnant of which was passing out of existence that night.

"Paul was our manservant," I replied. And felt the meanness, the disrespect, the betrayal—the sheer inadequacy of the reply, as soon as I'd given it.

I know what my mother would have answered. She would have said, with that faraway, slightly visionary, affectionate look in her eyes, "Paul was—Paul." Or: "You know, that's a good question." Or: "Paul was a lost person, I think—a displaced person." Or, in one of her particularly complicated maneuvers, that I have learned so well: "Paul was *wonderful*. I loved Paul, I really did. But you know, he really had a very sad, lonely life." Closer to the truth for her, though, would have been: "I loved Paul *because* he had a very sad, lonely life."

I have already mentioned that my mother was an empath, a romantic, and a sentimentalist—qualities I have absorbed from her. Accordingly, she tended to favor losers, even to ennoble them—and, of course, identify with them. On a number of occasions she confessed to me that she felt like a loser herself. I suppose at the time I was too young, or simply too credulous, to point out that for a loser she had done pretty well for herself. She had gotten out of Scranton; she had gone to New York; she had met, fallen in love with and married my father; they had moved to California, where he became a successful screenwriter; they had bought her dream house, where she lived for 34 years;

they'd been able to travel widely. And she'd been able to have a child—me (who would go on to write a book entitled *Failure: An Autobiography*, thus continuing the family romance, as it were, and enabling it to come full circle).

But the fact that I can now see the irony, and even the fallaciousness, in my mother's romanticization of losers, doesn't cancel out the fact that it made an impression on me which, like the impression of Tracy's seven-year-old hands in the concrete, has persisted to this day. I still can't help believing in the moral superiority of the loser, who will be vindicated someday (not necessarily in his lifetime—all the better, for this shows the timelessness of his cause). I recognize that this belief is not only seriously misguided, but hypocritical as well. Do I really see myself as a loser? Do I really want to see myself that way? And if I really were a loser, a failure—would I even be writing this book? There is much to the saying that the true voice of despair, of failure, is silent. (And the silent voice is certainly not mine!) It may be that I am, after all, only a failure manqué—a failed failure. Someone whose pretensions to failure, if one can speak of such a thing, have simply not been borne out by the course of his life. (That is actually what one agent, one of many—well over a hundred—who rejected this book, said: that I was not enough of a failure to speak authoritatively on the subject.) Let this, then, be the chronicle of a failed failure—and even, inasmuch as I have pursued failure, of a failed attempt at failure. But if this attempt did not succeed, it was at least in the service of a noble cause, and worth the try.

As a consequence of her favoring of the chronic underdog, my mother influenced the way I saw Paul. And not just Paul, but all "figures of failure," as I call them, who had a place in my life. Perhaps Frank, the much-abused cockney riding teacher at Kenter Stables, was also such a figure: a sweet, kind, mild-mannered man, having to do the bidding of the snooty horse-girls who treated him with disrespect. But such a judgment of Frank is probably not fair—after all, I only saw him an hour a week, for less than a year. I really didn't know him very well—not nearly as well as I knew Paul, with whom I shared a bedroom for several years. Paul, for me, was and always will be the definitive "figure of failure," in all his tarnished glory—a figure who came suddenly into focus one day when my mother and I were listening to the radio in the car. The Beatles' "Nowhere Man" came on, and as it played her eyes got that distant empath's look I knew so well, and that always made me mildly uncomfortable (probably because I empathized with it!).

"Does this song remind you of anyone?" she asked, with a contemplative little smile.

"Who?"

"Someone we know."

"We know a lot of people, Mom." I always tried to play down these soulful moments, because they embarrassed me. But what really embarrassed me, I guess, was that we were so often on the same wavelength. And I didn't necessarily want to be on the same wavelength as my mom. It was an intrusion. I wanted my own wavelength. I wanted my brain waves to myself.

"I was thinking of Paul," she finally said, and turned her shining eyes to me as the lyric sang out:

"Doesn't have a point of view,
Knows not where he's going to,
Isn't he a bit like you and me?"

"What!" I said, my voice instantly dismissive, my brain waves scrambling for a different frequency. "What are you talking about?"

"I don't know, I just can't help thinking of him whenever I hear this song. I'm probably just being stupid."

"You sure are, Mom," I said. "I don't know what you're talking about," I lied, and started fiddling with the power windows, which I knew really bugged her.

And now, of course, whenever I hear that song, I can't help thinking of both of them.

3

My Failure as a Friend

It was with my English friend Doug, while listening to the Beatles, that I first experienced the peculiar testicular response to music described in the previous chapter. I remember the exact time and location. We were in the living room with the French windows giving onto the terrace of the Villa Montgolfier in the south of France, in the summer of 1964. What were we doing in a villa in the south of France? The same thing, more or less, that we had been doing in England and India. My father was writing a screenplay, this time an adaptation of *Brave New World*. The producer of this project—which was never produced, at least not from my father's script—was based in Madrid, and my father was originally supposed to join him and write the screenplay there. But my father, no fool he, decided that summer in the south of France was preferable to summer in Madrid, and the producer agreed to this. So my father, on an expense account from 20th Century-Fox (those were the days!) arranged to rent, for that summer, an 18th-century villa about 20 miles outside of Cannes. It had been built by the brothers Montgolfier, the first men to make an ascent in a balloon (1783). (There's a little research! Very little. *Webster's Biographical Dictionary*.)

It was a fairy tale summer; I knew that even at the time. The villa, set on acres of grounds (tended by M. Jean, the caretaker) sloping down to the Mediterranean, had its own private beach, where we went swimming most days before lunch. Meals at home were prepared by Mme. Eugenie, M. Jean's wife, an erratic cook who was a little off in the head because of a wartime industrial accident in which her hair had gotten caught in a factory machine and her scalp had been ripped off. (The contemplation of this accident—which, as you might imagine, occurred to me not infrequently that summer—also produced an uneasy feeling in the balls.) The property included a cove of red rocks where we would go swimming in the afternoons. It was at this rocky cove that an octopus wrapped itself around my leg; I never went swimming there again.

Given the scarcely-to-be-believed beauty and opulence of the setting (which made the kind of suburban privilege I'd grown up with in the Palisades seem impoverished by comparison), it will come as no surprise that I experienced my share of testicular lightness that summer. Not only at the thought of Eugenie's accident (and it did not help—or perhaps in another sense, it did help—that she of the grievous head wound was also now our disgruntled servant; I guiltily felt that she should be relieved of all her duties to us), but also because of—well, because of the children of India, who had, of course, followed me to the south of France. They were with me often that summer: while bathing at the private beach, or off the red rocks (pre-octopus), or wandering the grounds while M. Jean and his assistants labored, or lounging on the terrace overlooking the blue Mediterranean. Or, for that matter, listening to the Beatles on the portable record player that Doug and I set up in the living-room, just behind the French windows that gave onto the terrace.

Of course, I breathed not a word of this to Doug, or even to my mother, to whom I usually confided everything that distressed me. But not this. This matter of my tender balls, brought on by the arbitrary, uncontrollable, and cruel juxtaposition of the music of "She's a Woman" with the mental images of the Indian children—this I kept to myself. And it was well that I did. Even Doug—loyal, steadfast Doug—would have been puzzled by it, maybe even have taken a dim view of it. It was bad enough for both of us that I was a bed wetter (until the age of 13!). The report of anything else suspect emanating from my privates might very well have driven a wedge between us that summer.

Doug and I had met two years before, when my family was living in London. Just around the corner from our two-story flat near Berkeley Square was a very different sort of neighborhood, a working-class neighborhood of tenement buildings: dirty-gray brick on the outside, industrial dark-green paint on the inside. I'd met Doug playing in the street one day. I guess I must have been on a walk with my mother, probably walking our Welsh corgi, Merrion (yes, we had a corgi, just like the Queen), since at that age, seven or eight, I wouldn't have been allowed to go anywhere—not to mention into a strange neighborhood—on my own. Once Doug and I got to be friends, however, I was allowed to walk to his building to play on those days when he didn't come over to our flat.

As inseparable as we were during my last few months in London, our friendship probably never would have been anything more for me than a "nice interlude" (part of my "English experience") if it hadn't been for my getting sick at the end of the summer, not long before we returned to the States. I was in bed with strep throat for at least a week, and Doug came to sit with me every day. My parents were struck by this show of loyalty and devotion in a child (Doug was only a couple of years older than I), and it became a kind of touchstone in our family. For the next two years we kept up by mail—Doug much more regularly than I. (That became part of the touchstone, too.) My awareness of Doug's superior conduct here was an early indicator of my consciousness of failure: He was not only a more loyal person than I was, he was also a more conscientious correspondent. No doubt my parents played their own role in this guilt-mongering by getting after me to answer Doug's letters, which I sometimes did and sometimes didn't. But despite my lack of full coopera-tion, the lesson was learned. In becoming the epitome of loyalty and conscientiousness, Doug came also to be a reminder of just how much I fell short of his example. Two of the three corner-stones of the Great Triumverate—failure and guilt—were thus laid in my first real friendship.

Two summers later, in 1964, Doug came to the south of France to stay with us at the Villa Montgolfier. The summer after that, he was with us on the Lido, in a penthouse apartment overlooking the lagoon of Venice, with the wondrous floating city in the distance. And then, two summers later, back in the States, in the Summer of Love, I failed him. And have believed, ever since, that by those actions of mine, the downward course of his life was set.

"Enough!" you say. "I have had enough of your rich boy's complaint! Enough of your spoiled-rotten whining about India, London, the French Riviera, Venice and the Lido. Your silver-spoon elegy turns my stomach. What do you know of true suffering, as opposed to the pseudo-sufferings of the pampered elite? What experience of anything worthwhile, genuine, authentic do you have, have you ever had, that permits you to speak of suffering? In this day and age of the evening-up of the playing-field—or at least of the wished-for, worked-for evening-up of the playing-field—what validating experience entitles you to speak at all? Why should I have to keep listening to you maundering on about this trash, with all the scruples, second thoughts, and gut-spillings of a privileged, spoiled little twit who was dragged around the world—if not kicking and screaming, for that would have been too authentic for you, then dragged squirming and moaning inside your portable hothouse, while your daddy cranked out obscenely overpaid Hollywood scripts, and your mommy, your Irish-Catholic bleeding-heart mommy, taught you, in spite of all her progressive intentions to the contrary, to be as guilt-bedevilled and paralyzed as she was. Why should I listen to your poor little rich boy's lament any longer? I've had enough! Give me some Studs Terkel, for God's sake!"

Don't hate me, reader. You shouldn't hate me, because the story of my failure—despite all the advantages of birth, money, upbringing, and education—to make anything of myself that would satisfy my own best image of myself, is virtually guaranteed to make you feel better about yourself. Not only because you will see, in my story, a poor little rich boy get his (in fact you have seen this already; you have already seen me at least beginning to get mine, through the medium of my prepubescent, killjoy balls), but also because, in reading the story of my failures, and of my general Failure, you will begin to feel better about your own. The story of my failure will provide a salutary cautionary tale for you, and will furnish you with the sort of nourishing hope that comes only from self-recognition: the recognition that while you may identify to some extent with me as a failure, your life, after all, is not and cannot ever be mine. You will do things differently, and perhaps learn from—and I hope be entertained by—my mistakes. In the end, you will feel that you have actually been rescued from failure—at least from my kind of failure—for the simple reason that, while you are me in some senses, in most you are not, and never will be. So you can therefore, in this question of self-recognition, both have your cake and eat it too. In the realization that it is my cake, and not yours, that has failed to rise.

Two summers after Venice, in 1967 (the "Summer of Love", ironically), Doug came to the States for the first time. I was 13, so he must have been 15. He had recently failed his O-level exams back in England, which meant that he would not be going to college, and his remaining secondary education would be vocational. The course of his life, in England at any rate, would then be fixed. In fact, it pretty much already was. Trade school, and then a trade. That, my parents explained to me, was the English system. The kids I had gone to St. David's with would be going on to "public school" (the English version of prep school), then university; but not Doug, because he hadn't gone to a school like St. David's. That was the way it was in England, and that was the way it would be for Doug.

Unless, that is, he remained in the States with us. If he stayed, he would go to high school in the Palisades and then, perhaps, on to college—which would not be an option if he returned to England. His future there was in the working class—like his father. If he came to stay with us, however, his future would still be open. He would get a high-school diploma, which would qualify him to go to college in the USA—or maybe even back in England, if he wanted (and if he could pass his A-levels). But one thing was certain: If he remained with us, his life from then on would be very different from what it would be if he returned to England.

I don't know for sure whether my parents had already talked this over with Doug before they broached it with me. I seem to recall that they hadn't, that they were laying out the idea to both of us at the same time, a day or two before Doug was due to fly back to England at the end of the summer. I do remember that they had taken us for a walk on the beach after dinner to present the idea to us. This memory stands out, not only because of the momentous nature of the talk we were having, but also because that was the only time I remember walking on the beach with both of my parents. It just wasn't something we ever did together as a family—which in itself now strikes me as rather odd, since we lived only a block up the hill from the ocean. But we walked on the beach that night. I remember the scene so well. The moon was up; the sky was clear; it was a warm evening at the end of August. I was feeling sad about the end of summer, anxious about the start of school—eighth grade, not quite as bad as seventh, but still not great, because I would be in Phil Thornton's class, and I was afraid of him. He wasn't exactly a bully, just an asshole, flicking towels at genitals and snapping jock straps in the locker room, turning guys around at the urinal so they'd pee on the guy standing next to them—that sort of thing. I'd spent a lot of time worrying about him in seventh grade, and didn't look forward to the prospect of same in eighth. But the worst feeling I had was about Doug's imminent departure: the departure of my best friend, who'd become almost like the brother I never had.

And then, all of a sudden, that night on the beach, everything changed.

Well, not quite everything. The summer was still coming to an end; school was still coming closer, stomach-clenchingly close now, like Sunday evening at the end of a long, rapturous weekend, with Monday morning looming. The long weekend had been the whole summer, which had included six weeks with Doug; and Monday morning was the new school year, just up ahead. But as sad as this all was, it was not unanticipated. Which is not to say I was ready for it. Who is? One day we are still free, as we have been for practically as long as we can remember (that is, since June), and the next day, the catastrophe is already upon us: the agitating trips for school supplies, the scratchy new fall clothes, the hideous and deforming before-school haircut—that harbinger of worse days to come, with the face that stares back at us from the barber's mirror looking cropped, already paler, no longer the carefree, tanned face of summer, and now weighted with the burden of autumn knowledge.

But much as I'd been dreading the end of summer, I can't say it was really unexpected. I'd even been preparing for the hardest blow of all—Doug leaving, for at least a year, maybe more. It was mournfully sad, but not unexpected, because it had happened twice before.

And then, all of a sudden, on that moonlit beach, he possibly wasn't going after all. The prospect I had been dreading most was suddenly put on hold, lifted from the horizon of expectation. Maybe he wouldn't have to leave; maybe he would never have to leave.

And just as suddenly as this possibility had presented itself, I knew I didn't want it to happen.

The reaction was immediate, the recognition certain; I didn't even try to conceal my response from my parents. From Doug, yes; I told him I needed a little time to think about it. But this didn't fool him; he knew he wasn't really wanted. My best friend—my almost-brother. Or so I had thought. But I was wrong; I had been deceiving myself. I had been an only child for 13 years now, and it was too late to change. Years ago, before I'd met Doug, I used to wish for a brother—even, sometimes, a sister. And when I had entertained the thought of Doug as my "almost-brother," it was more than just in name. What would it actually be like, one year, if he didn't go back to England at the end of the summer? What would it be like if he lived with us, not as a summer guest, but all year round? What would it be like if we went to school together? I'd gotten teased a lot in seventh grade, and I used to imagine him as my ally: how he would defend me against my persecutors; how he would fight on my behalf (he used to tell me about fistfights he'd gotten into back in school, how he'd licked the other guy); how we would fight together against Phil Thornton, and the Phil Thorntons of the world.

But now, that night on the beach, and afterwards at home, and in the day or two remaining before Doug left for England, I didn't even think of that. All I thought of was that I didn't really want anyone else. I didn't want an ally, a defender, a comrade-in-arms. I didn't want a brother anymore. And I didn't want Doug. I had thought I did; but now that it came down to it, I didn't. I knew I should have; I knew that I used to. But I also knew, with a surprising and dismaying certainty, that those earlier imagined scenarios of our possible life together were just that—scenarios. They were not real desires. And, what was even more surprising, I did not want them to become real. The intensity, unexpectedness, and certainty of my sudden realization took me completely by surprise. It was a dividing line, not only in my life, but in myself, separating me as I had previously thought I was—as I had imagined and wanted to be—from myself as I now recognized I was: selfish, possessive of my parents' attention, set in my ways, a creature of habit who wasn't going to let anything disrupt the life of self-absorption my parents had helped me create, and which they now proposed, with the best of intentions, to suddenly uncreate. Well, not if I could help it; and I could. Not for nothing had they had an only child.

Doug did not appear to be disappointed by my rejection of him. Perhaps because the proposal by my parents had taken him as much by surprise as it had me, he hadn't had time to build up any hopes, let alone expectations, and so could not be said to have had them dashed. But perhaps this is disingenuous on my part; surely he must have envisioned the possibility at one time or another, even if my parents hadn't said anything explicit to him. Perhaps he was more disappointed than I ever knew, and was just too good humored, or too stoical—or both—to show it. I will never know. On the few occasions when I have mentioned the memory of this incident, and my guilt over it—seeking his forgiveness, absolution, or just understanding of my actions that I myself have never been able to arrive at—he has dismissed it in an offhand way, as though the question of forgiveness, let alone absolution, hadn't even occurred to him (which very likely it hadn't), and the only thing that was important was to spare me unnecessary discomfort.

Doug is now in his 50s—unmarried, unattached (as far as I know), and suffering from a constant and apparently incurable facial pain. The doctors have not been able to find a physical cause of the pain, and medication hasn't really helped. Doug hasn't worked in years. He is an alcoholic, in and out of recovery. Both parents are now dead. He has an older brother, whom he doesn't see, and a loyal and attentive younger sister, Linda, who lives in the building across the street.

Years ago, he worked as a recording engineer, in England and South Africa. But he hated South Africa, and returned home. (This was in the 70s, under apartheid; though I cannot say whether apartheid was his main reason for leaving.) Then he left the recording business altogether—got fired, actually; he came in drunk one night and trashed the studio—and went to work in Selfridge's department store. But that didn't last either. Over the years I would get letters from him, reporting stoically, but always in good humor, never complaining, that he was in treatment for his drinking; that he was working, part-time, with the handicapped; that he was back in treatment; that he was making food sculptures (part of his art therapy); that he'd quit treatment; and then, the mysterious pain. The pain that wouldn't go away, and was getting worse. A couple of drunken phone calls, reporting—stoically as always, if it is possible to be both drunk and stoical; for Doug, it was—that the only thing that helped the pain was drink. But that relief didn't last either.

I remember saying to him during one of these calls that he should come over to the States for medical treatment; he could stay with us. My wife was not at all pleased with this; perhaps she was pregnant at the time, I don't recall. In any case, Doug had the tact, despite his pain (tact was always one of his qualities, along with loyalty, stoicism, and good humor), not to take me up on the offer. He probably sensed it wasn't completely sincere. And he was right; I never made the offer again.

How different would Doug's life be if I had agreed to the plan to continue his education back in '67? I have asked myself this question time and again over the years, and tend to give three answers. The reassuring answers go like this: "How different?

There is really no way of knowing" and "maybe, in the end, not very different at all." The other answer is: "Very different, and probably much better."

The years from 1967 to, say, 1970—when, in all likelihood, Doug would have graduated from Palisades High—would have been as different as high school in southern California is from vocational school in London. If he had then stayed in the States and gone to college, his life would have continued to be a very different life from what it was back in London and South Africa. Perhaps after that he would have returned to the U.K. and gone to work in the recording business, maybe even as a recording engineer. But then he would have been a recording engineer with a degree from an American college, and a foothold in the U.S.A. as well as the U.K. Perhaps he would have worked in the U.S.A. Become a resident, or a naturalized citizen. Gotten married, had kids, etc., etc.

All of that is—was—certainly a possibility: that the profound change in his high-school years would have put him on a very different course in life. But then so is the possibility that after high school, and even college, in the U.S.A., he might have returned to England and had essentially the same problems, and the same life. Since there is no way of knowing, since it is all speculation anyway, why beat myself up over it? Why wallow in guilt? What good does it do either of us?

There are no answers to the first two questions. But I do have an answer of sorts to the third, at least as far as the possible good that such idle speculation might do me. (About Doug I cannot say.) It is not a conventional kind of "good"; it is (characteristically) perverse, self-indulgent, contrarian. But it is nevertheless, for me, a "good," in the sense in which a prolonged inquiry into the question of my own failures can also be considered a "good." It is good to pursue the truth, even if it is not, finally, accessible. (As Freud once remarked, in his grand pessimistic manner: "The truth is not accessible; mankind does not deserve it.") But I don't believe that the truth in this case is inaccessible. Quite the opposite. It is all too accessible, and it is this: Doug's failure is my failure. Not only because his failure in life, if such it is, stems partly from my failure in the summer of '67 (the "Summer of Love"—ha!). But also because I share in his specific failures: his failure to be self-disciplined; his failure to have control over his own life; his failure to live up to his potential. To believe in himself. These are my failures too, as it turns out. Though I rejected him, long ago, as my brother, I have pursued, perhaps even embraced, our brotherhood in failure.

4

Failure at Exeter

In a recent issue of the *Exeter Alumni Bulletin*, whose quarterly appearance in my mailbox is always accompanied by a churning of the stomach and a sinking of the spirit, I read about two alumni who have changed careers in midlife. One of them, who graduated before my time (1969–72), is a newly retired investment banker and member of the Exeter Board of Trustees, who has now taken on the job of directing Exeter's fund drive from his home in Connecticut. The other, who graduated the spring before I arrived—but whose legendary tenure in the butt-room (designated smoking area) of A.C. Gillman House was still a topic of discussion throughout my three years at the Academy—recently left his position as CEO of the software company he founded, and is now a graduate student in Art History at Columbia. These are only two of a long list of highly successful Exeter graduates who have become rich and/or distinguished in their fields of endeavor, and about whom it is possible to read in every issue of the *Alumni Bulletin*.

And I do. Reading about them, and their achievements, is something I have come to dread. It is not so much them or their achievements that I dread as it is my own reaction to this information, which is as predictable as it is upsetting: a sinking of the spirit, a churning of the stomach, and the descent of the pall of failure upon the shattered remains of the day. This devastation, in turn, gives rise to a voice inside me, droning implacably: "You are a loser, you are a failure, you are an alumnus who will never be heard from again. You, too, were once a child of promise—promise that never came to fruition. What is wrong with you? Why have you failed? Where did you go wrong?"

Depending on my mood—which is never great after getting the *Alumni Bulletin*, but sometimes worse than others—I have various responses to this voice. On a good day, I can easily see the stupidity of the voice, and have no trouble rebutting it: "The set of values reflected in the *Alumni Bulletin*—the values, more or less, of the Eastern Establishment—are not my values. My values (which I learned in part, ironically enough, at Exeter) are Truth and Beauty, Sweetness and Light. Get thee behind me, Satan." On an average day, I say to myself, "I haven't failed. Nothing is wrong with me. I am who I am, that's all. What's for lunch?" On a bad day, I tell myself it all goes back to not getting into Harvard or Stanford, and *having* to go to Berkeley; to blowing my SATs; to my overall sense of failure at Exeter, which became clear to me in the potting shed in the spring of my senior year, when the college letters had all come in and I was on the losing end.

But to understand the emotions of the potting shed, it is necessary to understand the whole climate of failure, as it were—the climate in which I had moved for most, if not all, of my three years at Exeter. The climate of failure has many weathers, much like New England itself, with its seasonal changes, its seasons-within-seasons, its rapidly cycling daily variations. The general climate at Exeter, for me, was founded on the tacit sense of my intellectual inadequacy. My failure to quite live up to the high standards set by the Academy—and therefore myself. For I shared in the intellectual elitism of the place; it spoke to what was probably innate in me; it cultivated those early buds of the sense of failure, until they came to bloom in the musty, moldy afternoon warmth of the springtime potting shed.

I don't want to create the impression that I was unhappy at Exeter. I wasn't. Some of my friends complained bitterly about how much they hated the place. I would give an understanding smile and nod, but I did not really share their feelings. I did not hate it, ever—not even that miserable first winter—nor did I really understand, deep down, those who did. I was aware, of course, that it was much "cooler" to hate Exeter than to like it, and so I was careful never to appear to like it. But it would not have been possible for me not to fundamentally like Exeter, not to feel that I belonged there, if only because it appealed so profoundly to my vanity, my intellectual elitism, my wish for self-congratulation. After all, here I was, among some of the brightest kids in the country. How could I not have been pleased with myself?

The truth is, I wasn't. My self-satisfaction was just a cover for fear and self-doubt. Scratch the surface and you would have found an insecure and terrified teenager who didn't think he could make it through his first year at Exeter. Math was my particular terror—and that first winter, it was particularly terrifying.

This was no fault of the instructor, the kindly Mr. Jackson "Jack" Adkins, a spry gentleman in his 60s who pronounced his initial l's with a guttural sound, like French r's—"rramda, rrowest common denominator." After demonstrating a proof on the blackboard, he would say "mirrr-abile dictu!" and bounce the chalk off the back of his hand, catching it in his palm. I loved him. I was terrified of his subject, and he was endlessly patient with me. He made me use colored pencils for the geometry problems, as you would do with a child. He invited me over to his house for tutoring, and gave me hot chocolate. He also gave me a 9 on a test—out of 100—and underlined the score no differently, I noticed, than anyone else's. I understood that this underlining was not meant to call attention to my particular disgrace, but rather was a reflection of his spry, upbeat attitude: 9

was my honest grade, but let me not be cast down by it. Despite his kind intentions, however, there was no way he could give me anything higher than an E+ at the end of my first semester. (Exeter gave E's instead of F's, not only because it was alphabetically more correct, but as yet another expression of the institution's uniqueness.) As for that "+", it was a sign of Mr. Adkins' indomitable optimism, and I was grateful to him for it.

I had seen it coming. The first night back from Christmas vacation, I had lain awake all night long in my bedroom on the flight deck (top floor), certain that I was going to flunk out after my first semester, coming up at the end of January—or, at the very latest, by the end of the year in June. My room was the smallest in the dorm, next to the freight elevator, and made even smaller by the slanting insets of the dormer window, which projected nearly halfway into the room. I remember how the winter wind whipped past the window that night, and how the steam knocked endlessly in the radiator pipes as my mind, still on Pacific time, raced with various scenarios of doom, all of them involving flunking math and ending with my being requested to leave the Academy. There was no way I would be able to cut it at Exeter, colored pencils or no. (Actually, the childish pencils were just another sign that I couldn't hack it.) The fact that I was pulling B's in French and Latin was no consolation to me that night; I was convinced I would be asked to withdraw. Morning finally came, something like order was restored to my exhausted mind, and the direful scenarios receded as the problems of the day—of which math was still, as always, the greatest—took precedence. A week or two later, I became sick, and landed in the Lamont Infirmary, where I experienced a scenario of another sort, desolating rather than direful.

I had come down with the flu, and was running a fever, feeling achy and exhausted and generally miserable, though the feeling of elevation and detachment that also went with the fever was not unpleasant. My fever wasn't so high that I was delirious (though this also has its pleasures), but just enough so that things had an edge of strangeness to them, and I felt at a slight remove from myself. The feeling of being treated specially, and being exempt from the normal expectations and routine by virtue of having been admitted to the infirmary, was also not unpleasant.

Of course, the flu had its down side—not just the aching and exhaustion, but the sense of emotional vulnerability, the rawness of the nerve endings, which the feeling of disorientation brought on by the fever couldn't mask. I remember waking up very early one morning before dawn. There was snow on the ground. The sky was a bluish color I had never seen before, and absolutely clear—the bitter-cold clarity of a New England winter morning. It wasn't all that warm in the infirmary, either—they didn't believe in "coddling" the students, and the head nurse, a Nurse Ratchet type, was the embodiment of this philosophy. The scene outside—cold, foreign, strange, austere: the frozen snow, the old brick buildings with their tall white window frames, the bare-branched winter trees, the eerie blue atmosphere of the sky and snow—was a perfect expression of my feeling of homesickness and forlornness. The conviction fell on me once again that I was not suited for this place, that I would never make it to the end of the year, that I would never be able to pass math. The desolation and abandonment of the predawn winterscape permitted of no other outcome.

As it happened, I was right—that E+ was the best that kindly Mr. Adkins could do for me. But by the end of my first semester, when final grades came in, I had settled into the winter routine and was feeling less direful. My advisor told me I would have to bring my math grade up—which I did, to a mighty D+ by the end of the year. D was a passing grade at Exeter, though nothing to be proud of—but I was a little proud anyway, in spite of myself (partly because I had done it without colored pencils!).

But that spring I had other concerns besides math—spring itself, my first Eastern spring, and all the emotional turmoil that went with it. My upset centered around three things: chemistry, Kostos Peratikos, and Kent State.

In chemistry we were working on identifying the chemical composition of an unknown solution. This involved doing various experiments on the solution, using other known chemicals, keeping track of the results, and then making a deduction about the identity of the unknown solution. In junior high I had enjoyed chemistry because I liked chemical equations: The symbols and numbers were a magic language, not unlike the appeal of Latin, and later Greek (and later still, Sanskrit). The fact that the latter were all "dead tongues" only increased their fascination. I think my attraction to scholarship has to do with this same aura of romance, the atmosphere of the arcane and the recondite, seemingly hallowed by the scholar's participation in an elite guild. There is also, for me, a comforting quality in scholarly arcana—the comfort promised by all orderly systems. As a teenager, when I would smoke too much pot and become fearful or paranoid, I would recite (sometimes to myself, sometimes out loud) Latin and Greek declensions and conjugations in order to soothe my mind and reassure myself that I wasn't going insane. (Thus also the comfort of footnotes, bibliographies, and indices.)

In my first year at Exeter, I learned that the study of chemistry was a lot more than neat-looking chemical formulas (sorry, *formulæ*) and equations. It had to do largely with math, precise measurements, and lab work. The level of my success in these endeavors will be obvious to the reader. Though, since chemistry was not all math and lab work, and did involve some concepts and memorization (where would dreamy, unscientific minds like mine be without memorization?), I managed to squeak by with low C's. But my grasp of what I was doing in the lab, and what I was expected to do, and why, was minimal. This became painfully clear during the "unknown" project. The class was divided up into several small groups, and each group was to come up with a scientific deduction of what the unknown substance was. There would be a prize, or mock prize, for the winners. As it turned out, that wasn't my team, because when one of my team members asked me for one of the "known" chemicals to perform an experiment with, I accidentally gave him the "unknown" solution instead. Oops. His reaction may be divined. He did not try to conceal it from the rest of the class, who were also less than charitable in their response—though there was pleasure in their mockery, since my mistake meant that our group would have to start over from scratch, and thus was out of the running. Being a dummy was not something that was suffered gladly at Exeter.

The incident with Kostos Peratikos was a confirmation of this. A short time later, I was in the locker room talking with a friend, Jeff Brown, about Existentialism. I knew nothing about Existentialism, except what I remembered my mother telling me about there being no God, and life being what you made it. I told this to Jeff. Kostos Peratikos, who was eavesdropping on our conversation, and who was known to be a mathematical genius, said to me, with withering contempt: "That's not what Existentialism is, you fool." I can't remember if he went on to explain it to us; probably not (thinking we wouldn't have understood it anyway). But it wouldn't have mattered. I was cut to the quick. That Kostos Peratikos was also known to be an asshole did not seem to invalidate his identification of me as a fool—a judgment with which my classmates in chemistry would readily have concurred. I took it also as a slight to my mother, which made it even more painful. I could picture her eager face and hear her sincere voice explaining to me the apparently idiotic ideas that Peratikos had now dismissed and ridiculed in one fell swoop. That I was explicitly labeled an idiot was bad enough; that my mother was implicitly so was almost intolerable to me. But of course I could not defend her to Peratikos, however much I wanted to—that would have been insane: "Are you insulting my mother? Do you want to step outside, asshole?" But I felt just the way I had one day at the park when a kid came up to me and said, of the brand-new green Sting Ray my parents had just given me for Christmas, "You know, your bike is shit." I pictured their faces when I first saw the bike under the tree, and heard their voices, and it was all I could do to keep from crying in front of the bully.

That was also the spring of the Kent State shootings. A few of us were sitting in the Exeter Grill—the snack shop—talking about what had just happened. The self-appointed leader of the discussion was an upperclassman who was also one of the school's most outspoken political activists. In fact, he was one of the planners of the upcoming student boycott of classes, staged as a show of protest against the shootings and the war, and of solidarity with the students at Kent State. At one point in the discussion I asked a question—a very basic and probably dumb question, along the lines of "How many people were shot?" or even "Was anybody killed?" The student leader looked at me incredulously, then said, "What are you, illiterate? Don't you read the papers? Don't you watch the news?" (The answer to the last two questions was "No.") I was speechless, flushed with shame. This humiliation was worse than the chemistry or Kostos Peratikos incidents, because this time my failure was perceived to be a moral one. Apparently I just did not care enough to bother to inform myself that thirteen students had been shot, and four of them killed.

Soon after this, the boycott of classes took place. The leaders were calling on all students not to attend classes for the day, and to participate in the various protest events that were planned, including marches and teach-ins. Some of the faculty supported the boycott, some didn't. Hamilton Fish, my French teacher, didn't. He was aptly named, red-nosed and oenophiliac (to say the least). He was reputed to have married a DuPont, and to have once waxed rhapsodic, in class, about the joys of "spreading a lass's legs for the first time." (This quotation was passed around familiarly, yet with no diminution of its power to amaze, like a well-worn curiosity of nature. The remark occurred before Exeter went co-ed—though that probably wouldn't have stopped him either.) Mr. Fish lived in a butter-yellow house with black shutters in the middle of town, with a cannon and cannonballs (what else?) out front. On a bad day—and there were a number of those, unfortunately—his hands shook. His corrections on our exams were as florid as his complexion. He always surrounded each grade with a large red box. He let it be known that he would not take kindly to whoever chose to boycott his class, and would issue pink slips that would mean a trip to the Dean's Office, and some form of punishment. Nevertheless, most members of the class were going to boycott anyway, as we had determined before he entered the room the day before the boycott. What would I do?

I went to class. Not, as my classmates thought when they found out, because I wanted to suck up to Mr. Fish (though in my characteristic way I felt sorry for him), but because the thought of missing class for any reason at all, other than real illness, made me very uncomfortable. It seems to me that my conscientiousness was rooted in fear. Not so much fear of Mr. Fish, or what he'd threatened to do to us if we boycotted class (I don't remember if he ever followed through on his threat; he probably forgot). Rather, it was fear of a kind of corruption, of having my "academic virtue" compromised, of entering upon a slippery slope, the bottom of which was envisioned as sex, drugs, and flunking out. (About rock 'n' roll I was ambivalent: I liked listening to it and playing it, but concerts made me uneasy. The demonic energies unleashed during concerts were threatening, and I was always worried that I would somehow be required to do something terrifying, like ingest acid or have sex with someone (or both!). Or—which was almost as bad—that I would be ostracized for refusing to do these things.) From seventh grade on, academics in general served the same function as Latin and Greek would later on: They promised to protect me from the frightening anarchic energies of the outside world—specifically, the world of youth. I was afraid of the world of youth, which I had suddenly found myself thrust into in seventh grade, and turned to study for comfort and protection. The fact that academic performance was so emphasized at Exeter—more perhaps than at any other prep school, because of the "Harkness System" that kept classes to 12 or so students, all sitting around a seminar table with the instructor—only increased this tendency. I thought the demons of adolescence could be kept at bay if I mastered my declensions, conjugations, subjunctives and optatives, my passive voice and deponent verbs—not to mention the ablative absolute. Ah, the ablative absolute! Knowledge of these things made me feel not only smart and somewhat exalted, but also protected by the aura such knowledge imparted—as if studying Latin and Greek might create a sort of force field around me that would render me impermeable to whatever it was that frightened me (mainly girls, and what I might be required to actually do with them, as opposed to merely fantasizing about doing with them). Surely no harm could come to one who had mastered the various uses of the ablative absolute. I thought that there must exist somewhere a realm where knowledge of these things would be rewarded. In putting in my hours of study every day I was banking on a future payoff of the only kind that seemed of value to me—an intellectual or artistic one. It may be that even then I was preparing to be an academic, but I think the driving force behind my studying was less specific—and less trivial—than that. I imagined I was infusing my mind with large doses of the Good and the Refined (I saw them as one), storing up intellectual nourishment for some future unforeseen as yet. The sense of this destiny was as insistent as it was vague; perhaps it was its very vagueness that gave it its imaginative power.

It wasn't that I was not in sympathy with the boycotters. I too opposed the war, and had marched in a silent moratorium the previous October, during my first month at Exeter. Many of my friends were among the protesters now, and I felt a little guilty—but not enough to join them. I knew I would have felt even guiltier had I boycotted classes (think of all that knowledge, all that grammar and vocab I would be missing!). I also knew I just didn't care enough about the shootings to feel compelled to boycott. It makes me ashamed now to admit this—after all, kids

not much older than me, who opposed the war, just like me, had
been shot at, wounded, and killed, just for exercising their right
to protest. Did I really think a French lesson was more important
than that? No, I didn't. Yet the truth was that I didn't feel an
obligation to protest, either, whereas I did feel an obligation to
go to class. I knew I would feel even worse if I didn't go than if
I did. I also sensed, from hearing them talk the day before the
boycott, that many of my classmates were boycotting as much
out of peer pressure and nose-thumbing as antiwar feeling and
solidarity with the Kent State students, and this sense also made
me uneasy, and not want to join them.

And so I went to class, along with one or two other dweebs,
and faced the derision of the rest of my classmates afterwards.
We were suck-ups, chickens, traitors. Was this true? Maybe so.
That evening, in my room, the flood that had been building all
spring finally came, and I burst into tears. I told my roommate
and another friend all about my recent troubles. The assholatry
of Kostos Peratikos and the student leader were confirmed, and it
was agreed by all that I had no future in chemistry. The gratitude
I felt to my friends that night was kept a secret, but the tears I
shed came in response to their sympathy as much as anything
else.

At Exeter, after you turned 16, and with your parents' permission, you were allowed to smoke in designated "butt-rooms,"
usually located in the basements of the dorms and houses. You
could only smoke when classes or sports weren't in session: in
the evenings, after afternoon classes, on Wednesday and Saturday
afternoons, and on Sunday. On my 16th birthday, near the end of
the spring semester, I entered the butt-room of Wheelwright, my
dorm, and smoked my first "legal" cigarette. My roommate, Mike
Ward, was smoking a pipe, and I tried it. I immediately decided
I liked how it looked and felt to smoke a pipe. (I didn't at all like

the taste at first, but that was irrelevant.) I liked the *idea* of a pipe for me: It possessed the requisite combination of eccentricity, distinction, and excellence; it suited the image I had in my mind of the figure I wanted to cut. Also, my father smoked a pipe, and I liked the smell, and all the pipely paraphernalia. The taste, and the hot bite on the tongue, were at first only just bearable, but I bore with them, and in a few weeks, after my tongue and the roof of my mouth got used to it, I was an initiate.

That summer, back in L.A., I smoked constantly, and acquired a collection of pipes and tobacco. I wore an unbuttoned, four-pocketed, Brooks Brothers herring-bone tweed vest everywhere. In the pockets I carried several pipes (smoked on a rotating basis), tobacco pouch, pipe tool and cleaners, and a copy of Edith Hamilton's *Greek Mythology*. (I was psyching myself up for first-year Greek in the fall.) Pipes and ancient Greek seemed to go naturally together; they were the necessary pursuits of a votary of excellence, outward badges of an eccentric distinction. Several times a week that summer I would go to Ed's Tinder Box in Santa Monica (corner of Wilshire and Yale—no coincidence there!) to explore the many tobacco blends they offered. The store blends came in glass jars whose mixture the bespectacled and perennially puffing Ed supervised himself, and whose aromas, wafting from the jars when you opened them, conjured up an alchemical mystique, not unlike the letters of the Greek alphabet, into whose mysteries I was about to be initiated. I think the main reason I wanted to learn Latin and Greek was because of the magical element both of those dead tongues seemed to possess. Once I learned them, of course, they lost most of their magic, but retained their elitist cachet—which was almost as good for my purposes.

The commercial tobacco blends came in vacuum-packed ¼-pound, ½-pound, and one-pound tins. When you opened the tins, with a pipe tool or by wedging in and twisting a quarter (no other coin would work), there would issue forth a gratifying hiss, followed by the alluring aroma. Each mixture—"Morning

Blend," "Nightcap," "Dunhill Royal Yacht"—promised its own world, and supplied my imagination with its particular mode of being, an aura of suggestiveness and association that became part of the vague but compelling scenario that was playing itself out in my head. This scenario featured an idealized version of myself, both me and not-me, in various attitudes, signifying the old-fashioned heroism to which I aspired. I was the protagonist of my own drama, whose plot was not yet clear, but whose theme was nevertheless insistent: "Be Different;" "Rise Above the Crowd;" "Cut a Memorable Figure." (A self-dramatization that was an early, cinematic version of what would later become my habit of "biographization," where I imagine my everyday life as though it were the subject of a future biography.)

Underneath all the adolescent posturings of the pipe-smoking period was a frightened and insecure young man. Still a boy, in many ways, and most frightened of all about sex. My eccentricity played an important role here as well, for eccentricity seemed not only the *vademecum* of excellence, but was also calculated (though only half-consciously) to keep girls at a safe distance. I was afraid of sex: afraid of being unable to do it, of not knowing how to do it and, most of all, afraid that girls would think I was ugly and disgusting, and so would not want to do it with me, had I even been able or knowledgeable.

There was, I suppose, some objective cause for concern on this last point. My billy-goat goatee, and my reluctance to bathe, sometimes for weeks at a time in the winter at Exeter, certainly didn't help matters. Then again, it was so much easier just to masturbate into a sock I kept under my bed (the same sock, of course—also unwashed). Easier still to do it through my trouser leg, almost absent-mindedly, yet also compulsively, while reading Horace or Homer (in the original, of course). The leg of the trousers would then go unwashed as well, because the shameful and pathetic reason for its besmirchment was not allowed to be acknowledged, much less acted upon, by my "higher mind," whose business lay with the Golden Age Latin of Horace, the Heroic Age Greek of Homer—and not with the Teen Age deposits in my trouser leg.

God, what girl would have had me?

5

My Failure to Be Gay

It will come as no surprise to the reader that after the "Pipe-Smoking Period" came the "Gay Period." By "Gay Period" I mean that period of my life, starting with the summer after 11th grade (the summer after the Pipe-Smoking Period), when I not only thought, but even hoped, that I might be gay.

In the summer of '71 I saw two movies that had a powerful effect on me: *Death in Venice* and *Women in Love*. These movies spoke to the aesthete in me: the young master of exquisite sensibilities, set off from others, destined, consecrated—though exactly for what, remained to be seen. But whatever it was, it would certainly be excellent, beautiful, rarified, and distinguished. The Dirk Bogarde character in *Death in Venice* was who I thought I wanted to be—minus the passion for Tadzio. The business with Tadzio made me uncomfortable, yet I could also perceive its fineness, its nobility. Dirk Bogarde was clearly a fellow-traveler, except at a later, more advanced stage of the journey; he too was a votary in the temple of excellence, a pursuer of the unattainable, a figure tragic, absurd, and therefore admirable. Also, a natty dresser: the white linen suit and the straw boater were emblems of his difference, his dedication, his calling. The outrageous lipstick and makeup, donned absurdly and pathetically to attract young Tadzio, were a bit much, yes—but this was not a figure to be mocked. Only the great unwashed—no, strike that last!—only those who did not understand, who could not conceive of Dirk Bogarde's membership in a higher, better world, would even think of mocking him: philistines they, of coarse, unrefined sensibilities, not destined or consecrated, who knew not of the existence, let alone the meaning, of these mysteries. The fact that Bogarde's passion was a self-destructive one made it all the nobler, to my mind. In this corrupt world, the man of exquisite sensibilities was bound for destruction, one way or another; and the way of self-destruction—was this not the high road of the doomed heroism I found so attractive?

That, or some such, was what moved me in my confused strivings in the summer of '71. Not to mention the "Adagietto." God, the "Adagietto"! The exquisite slow strings movement of Mahler's Fifth Symphony, which provided the theme for *Death in Venice*, became also the theme of my inexpressible yearning that summer. I can't remember whether or not my mother had seen the movie—it seems unlikely she hadn't, though not with me. However, she too loved the "Adagietto," and recognized, without my having to explain, its importance in my pantheon. And how could she not? After all, it was her sensibility that in large part had formed my own. She had trained me, not by precept, but by example, to be responsive to beauty, suffering, and pathos. Hers was the sacred bleeding heart of the world—the "sacrum sanguineum cor mundi," I might have remarked ironically, puffing on my pipe; my irony directed not only at my mother's emotional susceptibility, but also at the déclassé Church Latin of the phrase. (For I was a "pure" Classicist.)

You may be thinking at this point not, Why did I think I was gay? but rather, How could I possibly *not* be gay? Only child, very close to mother—a mother who had, as several shrinks have since told me, "boundary issues"; a loving but distant father; a hothouse upbringing (literally, too: my mother raised orchids and other exotic plants in a greenhouse in the back yard). How could I have failed to be gay? Well, I did—but only just barely.

Maggie was the younger sister of my friend Dave Black, from San Jose, who had just graduated from Exeter. He was a year ahead of me, a writer and artist—three reasons for me to look up to him. The previous summer—the summer of pipe-smoking, 1970—Dave and I had gone on a two-week camping trip up the California coast, starting in San Jose and ending at the Canadian border, where we were refused entry because I didn't have a note from my parents (an embarrassing reminder of my minority status). But I'm sure that my eccentric appearance—wild hair, the billy-goat goatee, the smoker's vest full of accoutrements (let us not mention the trousers)—didn't help endear me to the Canadian border officials. They made a careful inspection of my pipes and tobacco pouches, sniffing and examining, then pointed us back onto the ferry, headed south. Our adventure, including my pipes, was immortalized later that fall in a story Dave published in the Exeter lit magazine, giving a substantial boost to my cherished reputation as a school eccentric.

It was just before the start of this trip, at Dave's home in San Jose, that I first met Maggie. Long blonde hair, kid-sister freckles, small white teeth, pretty pink gums when she laughed at my jokes. (Keep them laughing to ease the tension.) I remember being especially intrigued by the smallness of her teeth, and the pinkness of her gums; it was as though I'd never noticed these things before. (Well, maybe I hadn't.) She'd just finished seventh grade—or maybe it was eighth. She was learning to play the double bass, which towered over her, and which she bowed in bare feet (with painted toenails; they were pink, too). She'd just finished working on an elaborate diorama for school; I think it was of an American Indian settlement. She seemed like the perfect kid sister for my artistic friend—but not someone for me, caught up as I was with the romance of my pipes, and the vision of my style—which, as I've mentioned, were a kind of talisman against the fear instilled by such things as girls' pink gums and toenails.

I saw Maggie again when she came to visit Exeter the following spring; she was thinking of applying. She was with her mom, and they stayed at the Exeter Inn. I remember spending the afternoon with her, just hanging out, taking her on a tour of campus, and kidding around on a tricycle that must have belonged to one of the faculty kids. We had fun. I was acting silly, I made her laugh (the pink gums again), and I was glad to do that. She was my good friend's kid sister.

But that wasn't quite how she saw it. A couple of weeks later, when she was back in San Jose, she started writing to me, and I wrote back, still in the silly vein I'd established on the tricycle. Then, one day late in the spring, not long before the end of school, Dave came up to my room.

"There's someone on the west coast who wants to know if you've got a girlfriend," he said.

I remember the electric jolt that shot through me at the word "girlfriend," and the fluttery feeling in my chest that followed close upon the jolt. Me, a girlfriend! The concept was astounding—not so much that I should have a girlfriend (after all, this had been a blurry but insistent fantasy for years), but that I should be thought of (and by a girl!) as having a girlfriend, or as possibly having one. The fluttery feeling was also a kind of acknowledgment—simultaneously embarrassment and pleasure; maybe even the embarrassment of pleasure—that I was, after all, part of the human race. Why I should have been embarrassed to acknowledge this I haven't a clue.

Actually, that's not true. I do have a clue. I was embarrassed to acknowledge not that I was a human being, but that I was a sexual human being. Embarrassment at sex, and especially at the idea of sex for me. Not so complicated, really. Pathetic, but not that complicated. (And it has never really stopped being a problem.)

It was certainly a problem for me and Maggie. I let her down, in that regard. Worse, I humiliated her, in front of her own desire. I opened the door partway, then slammed it in her face.

I invited her down to L.A. twice that summer, once at the beginning of the summer, and once at the end. In between, I went to Europe, financed partly with the money from the Haig-Ramage Classical Scholarship that I'd won the previous winter. (And we know how I won that prize, don't we?) Framing that celebratory trip to Europe were Maggie's two visits to L.A., which should have marked another sort of celebration—the celebration of first love—but, as it turned out, didn't. I made sure of that. It wasn't just embarrassment at sex, at my own sexuality—the terrifying thought of real sex with a real girl, as opposed to a masturbatory and, so to speak, "classicized" fantasy—that nipped the relationship with Maggie in the bud. It was also my flirtation with my "Gay Period" that summer, and my (imaginary) entertainment of all the possibilities this entailed.

Not, mind you, the possibility of sex with boys: That was never part of the "Gay Period." I did not desire boys, I desired girls. But the thing about the "Gay Period" was that the desire for girls, for some reason, did not, to my very confused, classicized, Mahlerized, pipe-smoking adolescent mind, seem compatible with the "life of the mind"—as one of my classmates had put it, memorably, to me. "I want to live the life of the mind," he had pronounced one day after Greek class. This had seemed to me supremely admirable. And it was "the life of the mind" that I was now living, or thought I was living, or wanted to be living—or thought I wanted to be living. But how to reconcile the "life of the mind" with the life of girls? I hadn't a clue; so better to leave them out of the equation.

Whatever was in my mind that summer, I believed, in my ardently confused way, that I was not meant for a conventional heterosexual relationship. Such common fare was not for me. I was destined for something else—something finer, rarer, more complex, more distinguished. Not boys, maybe not even girls—but art. The life of the artist, the seeker: a life that entailed suffering, renunciation, and almost hopeless complexity. I also identified strongly with the character of Rupert in the movie *Women in Love*, played by Alan Bates (also, like Dirk Bogarde, gay). His drama, one of complex sensibility and searching, was the other important component of my "Gay Period" that summer. Rupert/Aschenbach/Mahler, *c'était moi*. Rupert's uncompromising fierceness, his strange attraction to the tortured and menacing Gerald (was Oliver Reed gay too?), his complex, troubled, and passionate relationship with Ursula, his sense of mysterious election—these all affected me strongly. And more than anything else, the surprising last line of the movie, spoken by Rupert, when Ursula says something like "Love is meant to be simple; people are meant to be happy," and Rupert replies, quizzically and abruptly, "I can't believe that." Then the movie ends. Wow. No truer, finer words were ever spoken to a 17-year-old's ears—a 17-year-old at once dreamy and diligent, rebellious and credulous, uncompromising and impressionable; words that echoed my own searching dissatisfaction, my desire for noble resistance: "I cannot believe that." Meaning, to me: I cannot accept that, I will not accept the thought that I was not born to struggle heroically, against all odds. I cannot believe that I am not, after all, one of the elect, destined to oppose, to resist, not to "go with the flow" (that contemptible acquiescence, so current in southern California at the time; and by the way—how did I ever come to be from Southern California, anyhow? There must have been some sort of mistake there.). *Never* to go with the flow—even to choose death ("at last, the distinguished thing"—but I hadn't yet read Henry James, either), rather than ignoble conformity. That last line of *Women in Love* was my rallying cry in my battle against the world.

And my relationship with Maggie inevitably became part of that battle. We should have been allies: Maggie and me, in love, against the world. Yet even that alliance would have been too conventional for me. The comfort of a relationship with a girl, which part of me wanted so badly—witness my shooting off into my trousers once or twice a day to the prosody of Homer and Horace—the pleasure and satisfaction that only a girl could provide were to be strenuously resisted.

Why?

For one, because I thought it would be too easy. Those things that were too easy were therefore contemptible, not excellent, beneath me and my noble mission (whatever it was), and so to be resisted and condemned. But another reason for resisting what was pleasurable and satisfying and "natural"—let us not forget to reject the natural, which was also too easy—was not because these "normal" things were too easy for me, but because they were too difficult. It was too hard for me, with all my affectations, to learn to be natural, and simple, and unaffected: too hard, and too frightening. The possibility that I was, in more ways than not, like most other teenagers—desperately horny, and lonely, and wanting to be loved—was just too frightening to me. My best defense was in erecting a bulwark of affectation—pipes, Latin and Greek, the cult of difficulty, even the possibility of gayness—through which a teenage girl could not, and would not even want, to penetrate.

The failed climax of this comic drama came at the end of Maggie's second visit to L.A., the night before she was to return to San Jose. I had somehow avoided, up till now, being alone with her late at night. We had had a makeout session at the end of her first trip, just before I drove her to the airport. It wasn't that I hadn't liked it—I had. We both had. She probably wondered what had taken me so long—and, after she left, so did I. But I didn't want to think about it too much, for fear of what I might find. Not that I was gay, but that I was scared—scared of sex with girls. What did that mean? That I was low-sexed? Sexually deficient, somehow? Asexual? But then, what was the meaning of shooting off twice a day? Was masturbation my preferred form

)parently so, at least to date. And was that the way it
for the rest of my life? Was I a lifelong onanist?

ast night of Maggie's second visit was different from
before. Not only because Europe (and Venice!) had intervened,
but because there was to be no third visit. It was the end of
summer. I would be returning to Exeter, starting my senior year,
in a couple of weeks. So this was it; there was no putting it off
anymore. (Most teenagers, of course, probably wouldn't have
thought of their sexual initiation in these terms; then again,
most teenagers probably wouldn't have thought of themselves as
Rupert/Aschenbach/Mahler, either.) Maggie had been sleeping
in the guest room, I had been sleeping in my room—the room
of my childhood and boyhood, since I was five. The room of
my virginity. But tonight, Maggie wanted me to stay in the guest
room, with her.

It was late, after midnight. We were lying on the rollaway
bed in the guest room, kissing. I could feel her heat through her
clothes. I knew what she wanted: me. And perhaps also to lose
her virginity, though I wasn't too sure about that. I never did
find out if she was a virgin or not, though I figured she probably
wasn't, even though she was two or three years younger than
me. I think she may have lost her virginity the year before to
Dave's friend and former roommate, Adam Feldman, an Exeter
boy wonder who was short and ugly and brilliant: poet, National
Merit Scholar, editor of the school lit mag that had published
Dave's story about our camping trip (but had never published
anything I had submitted. This, of course, was another sign
of Feldman's superiority—that he had rejected my writing.).
To me, at the time, Adam Feldman was the epitome of Exeter
brilliance. In the same issue as Dave's story, he'd published a
poem dedicated to Maggie. It seemed reasonable to assume
that the dedicatee had lost her virginity to the poet. Feldman,
whom I had known only in passing, was from White Plains, and
seemed to inhabit a higher realm than I: the realm of poetry,
genius—and Maggie. Maggie before I had known her. A Maggie

who, because she had been Adam Feldman's girlfriend, was a somehow different, inaccessible Maggie. But to Adam Feldman, she had been accessible; Adam Feldman would have known what to do that night. Was it really possible that she wanted me? Such thoughts—of the brilliant poet, of the two Maggies—on the rollaway bed in the dark guest room on this last night, after midnight, with Maggie lying on top of me, her body pressing achingly into mine, her groin, shockingly powerful, trying to fuse, through our clothes, with mine—such thoughts and feelings were overwhelming to me. She knew what she wanted, but I didn't. I didn't know what I wanted at all. Or perhaps it is fairer to say that I wanted many things that were as vague and elusive as they were seemingly noble. In any case, I suddenly and clearly knew what I didn't want: this. Not now. Not here, in my childhood home. It was all too much. I couldn't handle it, and I couldn't just let go, either—I couldn't just "go with the flow." Because it seemed to me that if I let go, I would lose myself, and never be able to find myself again.

So I attacked. Cruelly and gratuitously, I attacked. Of course, it didn't feel like an attack at the time—it felt like the truth. The "simple truth." I was simply "being honest."

"Maggie," I said, "do you love me?"

She didn't answer. Maybe she already sensed she didn't need to: either way, we were doomed. I would make sure of that. She didn't answer, but it wouldn't have mattered anyway.

"Because... I don't think I love you."

I was aware only of being "honest" and "thoughtful"—she deserved no less. In my mind, at the time, it seemed I was doing the "noble" thing, and therefore the right thing. In my mind I was probably smoking my pipe: puffing thoughtfully, contemplatively, aware—all too aware, and so totally clueless—of the figure that I cut. Determined to be a Rupert, an Aschenbach, to go against the grain, to choose—as I saw it—the difficult, the rare, the excellent over the easy, the unnatural over the natural.

Such were the rationalizations by which I rejected this lovely girl, this pretty, smart, funny, and willing girl who liked me. Maybe she didn't love me, as I feared, but she did like me, up until that awful midnight in the guest room. Until I "slapped her in the face," as she later told me, after I'd sent her a sort of love letter, or at least a veiled proposition letter, at the beginning of my freshman year at Berkeley. She wrote back, with gentle honesty—so different from my brutal version—to say she had a boyfriend. The shame I felt when I read her reply is with me still.

Yet although it would have been ignoble, to my mind, to sleep with Maggie that night, it also would have been ignoble to leave her. So I slept on the floor. It was just the gesture of self-punishment and self-abasement that I required. No doubt those emotions were also connected, in my mind, with nobility, or at least with the noble gesture: self-punishment, self-abasement, self-abnegation, all in the service of a higher cause.

And what was that higher cause, to my mind at 17? Homo-sexuality? My own perversely wished-for, imagined homosexu-ality? Not exactly; though in my sexual confusion and fear it might have looked like it. The higher cause that required both of our sexual sacrifice was the high priesthood of art. It had more to do with priesthood than with art, I now see—though at the time this idea would have been abhorrent to me.

That fall, back at Exeter for the start of senior year, the nobility of Rupert/Aschenbach/Mahler began to seem less compelling, and the sacrifice not worth it, as the memory of Maggie, her hot tangle of blonde hair, her pink gums and toenails, haunted my lonely Latin and Greek fantasies with the added sting of remorse. How could I have thrown it all away, in the brutal way that I had? And for what? I wasn't even gay! What, then, was I?

6

My Failure to Get into Harvard

Eberstadt. Just the sound of the name—abrupt, strange, harsh, even rebarbative; the clusters of consonants serving as a kind of synecdoche of the person himself, in all his uncompromising uniqueness—conjures up that entire period of my life when I was so much under his influence. "The Eberstadtian Period," I will call it.

"The Eberstadian Period" ran from senior year at Exeter—the fall of 1971—until roughly ten years later, after my wife Diane and I had just met. No coincidence there. Is it fair to say that Diane rescued me from Eberstadt? From the domineering power of his mind over my own? That mind was surely one of the most powerful I have ever known. It held sway over me for years, and I had trouble getting out from under it. According to Harold Bloom's theory of poetry, if Nick and I had both been poets—which in a sense we were, for a time at least, because we were in the same creative writing class—Eberstadt would have been the "strong poet," and I the "weak" one, my weakness showing itself, in Bloomian terms, in my imitation of his example, both literary and otherwise.

For instance: I imitated his obsession with "cripples." I use the word that he used, in all of its political incorrectness; for even in 1972 he reveled in being politically incorrect. I think his purpose in adopting this contrarian attitude was more political than cruel (though there was cruelty there, too). Undoubtedly he was political—though his politics, as I knew them, were cynical: the politics of *realpolitik*. I imitated the way he spoke: the clipped, blunt quality of his speech, which held equal measures of candor and cruelty. I tried to imitate as well the analytical brilliance of his intellect, but here I came up short, and knew it. For such brilliance, unlike a pattern of speech or a personal obsession, could not be imitated.

I could not escape his influence. (I was going to write "even if I'd wanted to." But that isn't true—I did want to; I just couldn't.) The dominion his mind held over mine was uncomfortable, and maybe even bad for me. Not exactly a "bad influence," but certainly not a beneficent one, like Diane's. Eberstadt was a major influence, but one that seems now—and perhaps even seemed so then, had I been paying more attention to its effect on me—to have been pulling me in a wholly other direction: the direction of power, as opposed to kindness; the direction of Exeter, where I met him; and of New York, where he was from, and where, when I moved there after college, we continued to be friends.

The entire phenomenon of Eberstadt must always in my mind be connected with the thought of my own failure. Why his success should have entailed my failure is as puzzling to me as why I should have held so firmly, and for so long, to the example of someone who was so profoundly different from me. I suppose that in the heat of my emulation I was not as aware of our differences as I later came to be. In any case, the perception of similarities and differences probably has nothing to do with why we take someone to heart as an example, especially in adolescence. It has more to do with the way in which they capture and hold our imagination. And Nick Eberstadt certainly did that.

He was tall and ungainly looking, with a long, horsey face,

incongruously full lips, somewhat thick wrists (associated, by me, with a sort of nonchalant cruelty—as when he would unconsciously dismember a chicken while eating it and talking), and the famously upturned Nash nose, seen also in his mother and sister. (Nash as in Ogden, his mother's father—another source of the Eberstadtian mystique, though not the main one.) With the ungainly appearance went a certain lack of physical coordination; he was, for instance, an enthusiastic but clutzy ping-pong player. The first time I saw him he was playing ping-pong in the Wheelwright butt-room. With his height and slight clumsiness, as well as his good-humored gamesomeness (the latter being another aspect of the aura of undeliberate, almost involuntary triumph that surrounded him), he made an immediate impression on me. But that first impression was without immediate consequences. I don't think he noticed me at all. Though it seems important to mention that there was never any aloofness or snobbishness about him; he was entirely too unassuming and self-confident—too strong, in short—for those signs of weakness. But I wonder: Is cruelty a sign of weakness? Yet his cruelty was not fundamental, only incidental—more in the nature of a nervous tic than a character flaw.

Eberstadt, as I really came to know him, dates from my senior year at Exeter, and actually not until the spring semester, when we were in the same creative writing class. A class in which he was, of course, the star—and in which I got a B+, the highest grade I ever got in an English class at Exeter. I took this in stride; I never expected an A, and it was only much later that this struck me as unfair. (And still does—surely the sign of a loser, to be smarting at a grade received over 30 years ago!) I am not sure that my final grade was not determined, in part, by Eberstadt's ringing response to my reading of what I thought was my best, or at least most ambitious work for this class, a long (too-long) story about an airplane mechanic at LAX who found enlightenment in a Buddhist bookstore in West Hollywood. "B+!" was the Eberstadtian verdict, delivered unhesitatingly (and triumphantly) right after I'd finished reading the story out loud to the class.

"I would have said 'A–,'" replied the instructor; but he ended up giving me a "B+" in the class after all. Nick, of course, got an "A." The pattern was symptomatic. I coined a term for it: "100–0." This was short for "100 percent–0 percent", which in turn was short for the idea that, whereas for most mere mortals, there was about a 50 percent chance that they would succeed in their endeavors at any one time, and a 50 percent chance that they would fail, in Nick's case, although it was certainly possible for him to fail, in actuality it never worked out that way, and he succeeded in his endeavors, dubious though they might sometimes be, 100 percent of the time, and failed 0 percent of the time. There was a celebratory aspect to "100–0."It was a sort of calculus of the Eberstadtian triumphalism, a make-believe quantification of my sense of his untouchability in matters of human weakness, matters in which I saw myself so very differently. When I commented, regarding one of his coups, "100–0," he would laugh and go along with it, not because he really believed in 100-0—he was too smart, too clear-headed, too practical-minded, too much of a "real-politician" to allow himself to believe in his own mythology, though I might—but because it was a shared joke between us, and because he enjoyed my humor. And also because he was assuming a role in our relationship. We both were. I was assuming the role of the loser, the schlemiel. It was a part I willingly played, because it made him laugh, and I wanted very much to make him laugh. Making Eberstadt laugh was a kind of badge of honor for me; it helped to raise me, I thought, in his estimation. (Though it probably served to lower me even more, by identifying me as self-denigrating, a clown, a buffoon. But if this was the case, better to have such a designation be self-inflicted, so that I could rationalize it and control it.) His laughter seemed to me to signal his knowledge of the part he was playing: that of indulgent royalty—noblesse oblige—to my court jester.

He did not require this self-abasement of me; I volunteered it. Which is not to say that he exactly discouraged it, either. The royalty in him, which is to say, after Arnold and Nietzsche, the aristocrat/barbarian, was pleased by the self-abasement of one of his underlings. Why, if it amused him, should he want to discourage it? What would have been the fun in that? And where would have been the power?

I have said that even then he was political. But that is not quite right. There were a number of people at Exeter who were more politically active than Nick. In fact, he was not really politically active at all, in the sense that political actions, positions, commitments per se did not attract his attention. What did attract his attention was power, the worldly power of which politics is the vehicle. This was why he was involved in student government. Not for "college suck," as we called it, but because student government was an aspect of power relations, such as they were at Exeter. And it was power relations that interested him. I had scarcely a clue about them then, and have not much more now. (Does this go along with the cultivation of failure?) But I did, in my intuitive way, sense something emanating from Nick, from his intellect—but which also went beyond his intellect—that I understood instinctually had to do with power: how it was used, and how he could use it.

It was this understanding of power, and the wish to understand it better, to study it and practice it, that caused him to manipulate people. He did not go out of his way to do this; but when the opportunity presented itself—as of course it often did in the intellectual hothouse of life at Exeter—he did not shy away from it. People would attach themselves to him—people like me—and he would welcome it. The more the merrier, as far as he was concerned, because of the opportunities for the observation and practice of power games.

I remember one boy in particular. I will call him Jacob Walden. Jacob had only one arm. The story, as I recall it, was that he'd lost his arm in a train accident, severed at the shoulder when he was messing around by the tracks and a train came suddenly around the bend. Jacob played the trumpet. He was one of Nick's attendants—and, like me, one of his favorites. Now, Nick was too smart, too sensible, and also too sensitive (though certainly he didn't always display or act on his sensitivities) to be condescending to Jacob. And Jacob was too proud to have allowed this, either. So what happened between them was even more remarkable for being so outlandish, for so totally overstepping the bounds of conventional "correctness" and entering another territory altogether. In regard to Jacob and his handicap, Eberstadt simply "dared"—and because he dared, he succeeded, and Jacob became "his," unquestioningly. 100–0.

Nick got it into his head one day to go about on crutches. And not just crutches. He went with one leg "missing." He folded his leg at the knee and tucked it into his trousers, which he then "pinned up"—just as Jacob would pin up his empty sleeve. The effect of this arrangement was that not only was Nick obviously "missing" a leg, but that there also protruded from his buttocks an outlandish "tumor," which was actually his foot beneath the seat of his pants. He went about campus like this for an afternoon, accompanied by Jacob, myself, and other attendants.

I remember the first sight I had of this procession, making its way down the Wheelwright staircase; and before the sight of it, the sound of it. A shrieking and a thumping were coming from the stairwell. The shrieking was of laughter—Jacob's; Eberstadt was silent, except for the thumping sound of him descending the stairs without the benefit of two legs. My room was at the bottom of the stairs, and I came out to see what the ruckus was. Eberstadt appeared on the landing, dragging himself the rest of the way (the crutches being of no avail here; someone else was carrying them, maybe even Jacob). The shrieking continued, now joined by myself. Nick was still silent, wearing only his characteristic bland smile—a smile that seemed to acknowledge both that he was, as usual, at the center of the hurricane he had created, and that he was disavowing (disingenuously, but conscious of his own disingenuousness; his knowing cynicism was also part of the joke) the actions of the people around him. The bland smile was the sign of 100–0 in action: this whole spectacle would somehow end up not getting him in trouble, not even with Jacob. More than that, it had Jacob's sanction. Even more, Jacob *liked* it. Jacob was having *fun*. Nick's antics were amusing him. Nick was playing the buffoon for his entertainment. That was the only way this monstrosity could have happened in the first place—with Jacob's sanction.

But just how *had* it happened, and what did it mean? Had Nick presented the idea beforehand? "Hey Jacob, what if I tuck my leg into my pants leg and get a pair of crutches and go around like that?" How had he gotten the crutches, anyway? Probably from the Lamont Infirmary. Stolen? Perhaps. Borrowed? Less likely. ("Nurse, I just need to borrow these for a little while; I promise to bring them back." No, that was not nearly bold enough; and Nick was nothing if not bold. 100–0 favored boldness, not caution. Caution got you caught; boldness got you away with it.) More likely he had them already for some injury. But how he came upon the crutches doesn't matter, and is only another aspect of 100–0 in operation: He had the crutches, and was now making "good" use of them. (The Eberstadtian use of the word "good" was in itself a complicated case, and required that quotation marks actually not be indicated—at least not by him—when more conventional moral sensibilities, like mine, would have employed them to signal an ironic use. Eberstadt needed no such signals; his wish was to confound the conventional, and its slaves.)

"And oh yeah, Jacob, you can hold the crutches when I go down the stairs."

"Yeah, sure, Nick. That sounds like a good idea."

Was that how it went between them? Was that how the idea was conceived? And what about the motivation? And what did it all mean? I mentioned that Nick had been writing "cripple stories" in creative writing class. These stories accounted for a large portion of his output. Such efforts would now come under the heading of "juvenilia." And I remember that when Nick, probably through family connections, sent some of his stories to an editor that spring, he was told as much—that they were juvenile. He announced the news matter-of-factly to me, perhaps as a necessary corrective to what he sensed was adulation on my part.

And it was. Almost total adulation. It wasn't just that his writing did not seem like juvenilia to me at the time. That would be like saying that your first crush did not seem like puppy love at the time. Of course it didn't. Though considering the intellectual snobbery so prevalent at Exeter (a snobbery that I lapped right up; it was of a piece with my pipes and my would-be "gayness"), such an awareness of juvenilia, even one's own, would not have been all that surprising. For a kind of affected hyper-consciousness went along with the kinds of snobs we not only aimed at being but actually were.

It now seems to me that snobbery of one sort or another goes hand in hand with my sense of failure. But there was something more objective, too, that prevented me from seeing Nick's writing as juvenilia, and that was its undeniable power. He wrote sentences, and sometimes even whole stories, of a pared-away starkness that seemed beautiful to me. His sentences, like his speech, were often clipped; but in writing they did not seem glib to me because they were in the service of something else, something larger and greater, I thought. They were in the service of suffering, sadness, and an unsentimentalized compassion—precisely those qualities that I wanted and labored to achieve in my own writing, and that Nick seemed to produce so effortlessly. No doubt there was a good amount of projection in my response to his writing, but there was also a solid wall of undeniable talent for me to project onto: a good ear for the language, a gift for succinctness (how I envied that, and still do!), a harsh but clear vision of the realities of the world. My writing was full of wishfulness and sensibility, focusing on characters put upon by the world; Nick's was full of the actualities of the world. We both wrote about victims, and here I also followed his lead—though without "cripples," and with very different premises. I sympathized and empathized with my victims; and while Nick did this to some extent, his interest was more in the forces that victimized them. There was also the fear, just below the surface of his writing, that there but for the grace of God went he.

Yet right alongside the vein of cruelty and deliberate political incorrectness ran a softer current. He could be kind and sympathetic at the drop of a hat.

When I was feeling down and out one day (probably relating to my college rejections), Nick noticed my mood and asked what was wrong. I told him I was feeling blue, and that to these feelings was added self-reproach for feeling this way, since Bob Friedman, another math genius (but much nicer than Peratikos, and a friend of mine), to whom I'd earlier told my troubles, had said there was no reason to feel depressed: I was smart, educated, funny; I would do fine in life. There was no reason to be sad.

"That's bullshit," Nick replied. "Everybody gets depressed from time to time. Tell me about it." I did, and he listened, in that attentive, serious way he had, head cocked down and to the side, nodding, fingers cupping his chin. Without dismissing what I was saying or feeling, he told me, with the assurance of a doctor, that I'd probably feel better tomorrow—which I did, largely because, rather than adding to my burden, as Bob had done (though unintentionally), Nick had lightened it just by showing sympathy.

That was another one of his gifts—psychological insight, the ability to read people correctly, and respond accordingly. It was a gift that cut both ways, for it also enabled him to play power games skillfully, and to act self-servingly and manipulatively. But the impulse toward big-heartedness was there, and he was not afraid to show it. I remember being with him once on a bus in downtown Boston. A man on crutches (or "cripple," he would have said) was struggling to sit down, and was about to fall. In a flash, almost before I'd had time to register that there was a problem, Nick was up and helping the man. He said nothing afterwards, because there was really nothing to be said. He had seen what needed to be done and done it, without any doubt or hesitation.

I have never forgotten this little incident. It seems to point simultaneously to Nick's strength—his power of action: in this case, right action—and my weakness: knowing what needs to be done, what I should do, and even what I want to do, but—for one reason or another—not doing it. Thinking too much. Inhibiting myself from acting on my instincts. And also suffering from something peculiar to my relationship with Nick, which amounted to being overwhelmed by his example: by his single-minded yet intelligent certainty, his instant recognition of what needed to be done, and his unhampered ability to do it. That's just it: Where I was hampered—by scruples, doubts, hesitations, self-consciousness, embarrassment, fear of what others would think—Nick was, or seemed to me to be, supremely free of those fetters. He was perhaps the only person I knew who possessed both intellectual brilliance and the ability not only to understand power but to wield it. Because of this ability, which he understood was more important in the world than pure intellect, he did not consider himself an intellectual, nor did he really respect intellectuals. In fact, he used the term derisively. Nick valued ideas for their usefulness in the world, their relevance to the exercise of power. If this makes him sound chilling, he could be. I had never met anyone like him before, much less become friends with such a person. I was unable to keep from being overwhelmed by the power of his mind, and I was also flattered and grateful that he considered me a friend. My friendship with him raised myself in my own eyes (and also, I believed, in the eyes of others), and seemed to do for me, in the personal realm, what the study of Latin and Greek did for me in the intellectual realm. It provided a reassurance that was elitist, protective, self-congratulatory, and confirmational: surely by my mere association with a friend like Nick Eberstadt I was destined for great things. Our friendship was surrounded, in my mind, by a golden aura of election—the special illuminating light of Exeter, immune to the vicissitudes of the world outside the Academy. Yet I never felt at ease around him. How could I, with so much riding on our friendship, as I imagined it?

One of the biggest things I was hampered by, and which he seemed entirely free from, was guilt about his own privileged status in the world. I think Nick saw clearly how guilt poisons one's actions, and so would have no part of it. His emotional make-up was such that his "guilt organ" was not so highly developed as mine. Furthermore guilt, when it came to him (as I'm sure it did, from time to time—despite his cruel streak he was no brute), was not a feeling that Nick would allow himself to entertain. He once wrote me, in reply to an anguished letter of mine: "I bury my neuroses. You try to make them grow."

In the spring of senior year I was part of the "Work Program," which allowed you to get out of sports by doing various menial jobs around campus, in conjunction with the grounds crew. Several of my friends—Nick, Bob Friedman, and Chris Robinson (a highly eccentric classics genius, and thus another figure of emulation for me)—were doing the Work Program, and so I did, too. These were three of the brainiest guys at Exeter. I was totally out of their league, and secretly prided myself on the fact that they would even associate with me. With my pride, of course, came a strong dose of inferiority, which I tried to mask by playing the clown.

One of our jobs that spring was cleaning out the potting shed behind the art building. We must have spent a week or so at this task—sweeping and throwing away broken pottery shards, stacking and rearranging the good pots, maybe even doing some minor repair work on the rotted lath shelving. I remember some broken windows, too, with the warm spring sun coming through. It is unlikely we would have spent only one afternoon working in the potting shed, but that is how I remember it: one afternoon, a hot, sunny afternoon in late spring of my senior year at Exeter. A time that might have been, that should have been, a time of triumph for me as a graduating senior, bound for college after three years of grind. (I was a diligent student; I had to be.) A time that I'm sure was a time of trimph for Eberstadt and Friedman, boy geniuses headed off to Harvard. (Chris would go the following year, on a scholarship.) But for me, there was no college triumph. My letters from Harvard and Stanford had both been the dreaded thin letters of rejection. I hadn't made the grade; my friends had. I was going to Berkeley. Nothing to be ashamed of, I know that now. But at the time, I didn't; and I was very much ashamed. It is hard to say which was greater for me that spring, the shame or the heartbreak. But why stop there? There were also sharp feelings of inadequacy, of not-quite-bright-enoughness. (The proving ground of Exeter was very good at inculcating these, at least in those such as me. Perhaps the friendship with Nick, Bob, and Chris was, in part, my attempt to prove otherwise.) The long-awaited beauties of the New England spring, my last at Exeter, made these feelings all the more intense and bittersweet. And the atmosphere of the potting shed—hot, musty, loamy, with the elegiac late-spring sunlight slanting in through the broken windows—seemed to condense all of my heartbrokenness into a single scene of misery.

This light, as I remember it, was inseparable not just from my misery, but from the schools that had caused it by rejecting me. The fact that Nick and Bob, Harvard-bound—headed for "the fair courts of life"—were also working with me in that potting shed was a cruel reminder that they had attained, by virtue of their superior abilities, to what remained (and always would remain) unattainable for me: Harvard. Those two distinguished, quintessentially eastern syllables connoted so much—perhaps nearly everything—that was of value to me at that time. The spring light of the potting shed betokened the unattainability of Harvard, of the true "life of the mind"—these things gaining a hold over my imagination and desires in direct proportion to my exclusion from them. For surely, it seemed to me then, such a life could really not go on anywhere else; surely not at Berkeley, where I was headed, and which to me, compared to Harvard, represented a fallen state.

The light of the potting shed was also the light of someone else's triumph—Bob's and Nick's. Through my piercing disappointment, and partly because of that disappointment, I was especially aware of their success. I could feel how what was for me the light of unattainability was, for them, already the light of attainment. They were resting in the sunlight of being Harvard-bound; I had been rejected, and was lying in a corner, in the shadows. In the midst of my own failure, I could feel their triumph, Bob's and Nick's, and so my failure became all the more bitter by contrast. I envied them; perhaps I even hated them for a while. And if I did, it would have been that day in the potting shed that my hatred first made itself felt. But the feelings of hatred didn't last, because they couldn't hold out against my much stronger, and self-directed, feelings of inferiority, the confirmation of my self-doubts. The long ride of hope that I'd been on since the beginning of senior year was now over, had come crashing to a halt. And it was only now, when the gates to the kingdom were finally closed to me, once and for all, that I fully realized how much I had longed, all along, to be admitted to Harvard. To go there too, I suppose—after all, my father had gone there—but even more, to be *admitted*: to be among the blessed of the Earth, granted access to the fair courts of Harvard College. All of the previous fall and winter I had nurtured hopes. How could I not? I was no dummy. I "had" Greek and Latin. At Exeter, no less. ("Exeter Latin" and "Exeter Greek," so named by my instructor in both, the formidable Mr. Coffin, were a source of no small pride and self-satisfaction to me, a mark of distinction on which I preened myself.) I had made High Honors one semester, and was a recipient of the "Haig-Ramage Classical Scholarship," which had partly paid for my trip to Europe the previous summer. And so as January dragged into February, and February into March, those hopes grew. Images of myself at Harvard, magically transported in a feat of elitist legerdemain from L.A. to Cambridge, and there embowered in the fair groves of academe—the fairest of all academic groves—such pipedreams were irresistibly nurtured by my wishful imagination. So when the college letters arrived in mid-April, it was the Harvard rejection that hurt most of all. (Despite its mitigating qualification, letting me know that I'd been put on the waiting list. I knew that being put on the waiting list at Harvard was about as hopeful as being put on the waiting list for the lottery.) The pain of rejection took me by surprise—not so much the fact that I didn't get in (the failure in me had always known, deep down, that I wouldn't get in, that I wasn't good enough) as how much it hurt not to get in. The knowledge that Nick and Bob had gotten in brought the added emotions of envy, inferiority, and temporary hatred to the pain I was feeling (a sort of reverse La Rochefoucauld: "It's not enough that we should fail; what we really don't want is for our friends to succeed"). The fact that my father had gone there brought shame as well.

The pain of failure that spring was displaced not only onto persons—Nick, Bob, my father—but also onto things, such as the potting shed, and the chorus rehearsal for the spring production of *The Mikado*. (Another job of the Work Program was to sweep out the newly constructed Fischer Theater, where the cast was rehearsing.) Though to call this process "displacement" seems too abstract and theoretical. Let us say, then, that the potting shed outside the art building became a scene, a locale of my pain, as did the chorus rehearsal for *The Mikado*. Specifically, it was the opening lines of the show, with their succession of repeating notes: "If...you...want-to-know-who-we-are/We...are...gentlemen-of-Japan," as well as the afternoon light slanting into the potting shed, that became emblems of my heartbreak—elitist, privileged, poor-little-preppie-boy heartbreak; but no less painful for all that.

Over 20 years later, when I moved to Massachusetts with my wife and child, I recognized that same light again; yet how different was everything else. It was 1994. I was married to Diane. We had a son, Zack, who was almost seven. And I was now a college professor, starting my first full-time teaching job at Holy Cross, in Worcester—the school I'd had my heart set on all through the previous winter and spring (long-ago shades of the Harvard longing!), and where I'd been hired only six weeks before as a sabbatical replacement. Within the space of those six weeks, Diane somehow managed to orchestrate the transcontinental move from L.A. to Worcester (those two places so diametrically opposed in just about every way, starting with the geographical; that diametrical opposition had been a theme in my life ever since Exeter), while at the same time finding a school for Zack, and a place for us to live. The time of year we arrived in Worcester was not late spring but late summer; yet the light was the same I remembered from Exeter, many years ago. "*Quantum mututus ab illo…*" murmurs my Exeter Latin (Vergil). "How much changed from the one who…." In an ironic reversal that was gratifying to contemplate, the clear New England light now brought not misery and self-denigration, but a sense of poetic justice. What goes around comes around. Rejected by Harvard, yes; but now I was a college prof at Holy Cross (those syllables as exciting to me now as "Harvard" once had been)!

A number of times during our three years in Worcester, we would drive into Boston or Cambridge for a night out. Usually we would get a babysitter for Zack, but on one particular evening Zack was with us, and had brought a friend. It was a clear, cold winter evening, and there was snow on the ground.

A quintessential Harvard scene. We had gone to John Harvard's Brew House for dinner. Making our way back to the car, we took a little detour through Harvard Yard. As we walked through the Yard, always and still a place of legend to me, I could not help feeling a pang—the pang of rejection remembered (the potting shed pang), but also the pang of exclusion—lifelong exclusion from membership in this place, this scene I was walking through. Many of the students on the snowy streets and pathways of the Yard were the age of my students at Holy Cross—a whole academic generation removed from me. How could I possibly be feeling inferior still to these youngsters? But I was. They were still, would always be, for me, among the blessed of the Earth. And I was not, and never would be, among them. The brick buildings on the Square and in the Yard, the tall latticed windows lit up from within to signal the life, studious and otherwise (probably otherwise, since it was a weekend), led by the blessed denizens within, reminded me of the buildings at Exeter, and similar winter evenings there. The same architecture: brick with white-trimmed windows (some of them semi-circular on top; those must be lecture-halls, or churches), dormer windows on the flight decks of the dorms, slate roofs. It was Exeter, of course, that had been modeled after Harvard. But the type was the same, the world the same. I had once been part of that world. And here I was again. Not part of it anymore, yet not wholly removed, either. I was teaching at a college in New England, after all. A long, long way from L.A., and not just geographically. A sense of space and time traversed, long distances of experience passed through, great expectations undergone, disappointed, some of them (such as my academic career) curiously fulfilled, or on the way to being. (The Holy Cross job story was one such sequence of events, during that first unforgettable, crucible-like year on the academic job market. See Chapter 10.) An unexpected feeling of pride now went along with the feeling of exclusion and remembered pain as I walked through this small corner of Harvard with my wife and son. The sense of failure this place aroused in me was less insistent now (though never entirely absent; covered over rather than eradicated; it will never be eradicated). Yet that failure had been necessary to produce this moment of quiet triumphalism. A moment in which failure was recalled and transmuted—not into success, but into something like survival and endurance, which are more lasting and profound than success. This moment consisted of a number of different things experienced all at once: the "Harvard tableau," seen "of a winter's evening"—snow on the ground; indigo sky above, with a few bright, cold stars; warmly glowing windows indicating (and, to my envious imagination, celebrating) the blessed denizens inside—the whole cozy self-containment of the place, which someone less reverential than I regarding these things would probably call "smug." The smugness of Harvard, and what it represents. True enough—and yet that is not the end of the story for me, the boy in the potting shed, the sweeper at the theater, overhearing the strains of *The Mikado* that spring of his heartbreak. (How many in that cast, I remember wondering, were going on to Harvard next year, and so were "set"?) That boy, who had somehow become a man, with a wife and son, saw it now not as smugness, but as an enviable snugness, the snugness experienced of a cold winter's evening. (The "of" here is *de rigueur*, a necessary archaism when speaking of such romanticized things.) The snugness of it all was to be registered and appreciated—but only from the outside, by the failure, by the one who was excluded. By me. Because the blessed denizens could not see themselves, since they were inside the buildings. Of course, it was entirely possible for a blessed denizen to be walking outside, and to be having such thoughts as I was now having. Possible, but not likely, because blessed denizens were not and never could be outsiders in the second sense—they were students in Harvard College, they had triumphed, they were in, they were "set." It was only from the perspective of an outsider, of a nondenizen, of a rejectee—of a failure, in short—that one could truly appreciate the snugness and the pleasingness of the Harvard tableau, of the fair courts of life.

7

Failure in New York

I came to New York the October after college with a copy of *Bleak House* to read on the plane, which I slogged through for maybe a hundred pages before giving up. It was *Great Expectations* I should have brought, of course—though it wouldn't have mattered, because I wouldn't have gotten any farther in that, either. It was really only the title that I needed: the sense of a great journey underway, of home left behind, of the larger world awaiting me, and all its glittering prospects.

On the red-eye from LAX to JFK I sat next to an actress in her late 20s, who'd had some roles on TV (she was coming back from a shoot), and who lived in the east 30s, in Murray Hill. She slept for part of the trip, but I was too excited to doze for more than a few minutes at a time. (Maybe a little of that excitement came from having an attractive older woman sleeping next to me.) I tried in vain to apply myself to *Bleak House*, but its only purpose, besides killing time in a (wishfully) edifying way, was to serve as a kind of receptacle for my high anticipation, whose images and hopes I would pour, as it were, into the pages I was looking at but unable to absorb. It seems to me that this is often the function of books, magazines, and movies on plane flights to eagerly anticipated destinations. Unbeknownst to us, they become part of the imaginative voyage (which is always the best part of the trip), their content almost totally overwritten by our excitement and expectations. Whatever story they are trying to tell, whatever information they are supposed to convey, are surrounded and soon forgotten by the emotional context in which they are received: our sense of being launched into a significant new experience, a new era of our lives. *Bleak House,* on that red-eye flight to New York, was such a book for me—barely comprehensible in terms of its overt content; but then its overt content had little to do with its meaning. It was a *vademecum* on the passage from my past into my future; from the West Coast to the East Coast; from minority to majority; from studenthood to livelihood.

We landed at JFK not long after dawn on a clear October day. I hadn't been up so early for many years. But then I hadn't really gone to sleep, either, which only added to the morning's discombobulated effect. The actress knew of a shuttle bus from JFK into Manhattan that was cheaper than a taxi, so we took that, moving towards the towering wall of eastside Manhattan, shining in the morning sunlight, then down through the Midtown Tunnel, from which we suddenly emerged in the middle of Manhattan, in all its dense, rich plenitude. I had arrived. The sense of particularity of place, of an unimpeachable New York genuineness of being ("This is reality, finally!") was overwhelming: bricks, grime, rusted metal, potholes, horns, yellow taxis, city buses, the smell of diesel (which always reminded me of winter visits to my grandparents), the clear blue October sky above the dirty but dignified buildings—they had none of these things in L.A., at least not in the particular way they had them in New York. Nothing else came close to this, my racing heart assured me. I knew that what I was feeling—that this was the start of my grown-up life—was what countless others had felt before me, but that didn't matter. It was still happening to me, this strange new morning in this mythical but real place that was, after all, not a new place to me, but that I was seeing now with new eyes, at a new time of day, in a new chapter of my life.

The actress and I took a cab from wherever the shuttle bus stopped—I think it was Grand Central—to her building in Murray Hill. She offered to split the cab fare with me, but I gallantly refused, saying I would take her phone number in lieu of payment. She laughed, with an edge, and deftly replied that I was a little young for her. I must have blushed then, not so much at the embarrassment of rejection as in surprise at my own boldness. I had never asked a virtual stranger for her number before. That, too, was something new today.

The cab continued up Madison as I sat back and excitedly drank in the sight of the elegant shop windows sliding past: men's and women's clothing stores, shoe stores, leather-goods stores, luggage stores, cutlery stores. There must have been jewelry stores too, but they would have been almost redundant to my senses right now, since Madison Avenue itself seemed like a jewel in the early-morning light: rich and fancy and snooty and alluring, like a sophisticated Manhattan woman in her prime, or just after, in pearls and pampered skin, fascinating and instructive—and by whom I intended to be instructed. I was still feeling a buzz from my boldness with the actress, as well as the little sting—not entirely unpleasant, a mark of my emerging adulthood, I thought—of being put in my place.

The excitement of arrival crested as I rang the doorbell of 111 E. 64th St., my grandmother's house. I rang it again. And again. And again. The cab had pulled away, my suitcases were in front of the door, and still no answer. I stood there ringing for about five minutes, until it became clear that she wasn't going to answer. Maybe she was still asleep (though she had always been an early riser, and she knew what time I was arriving). Maybe she'd stepped out to get some frozen waffles. (She always gave me waffles for breakfast.) Or maybe....

By now the edge had come off my excitement, and anticlimax

had given way to worry. I walked over to Lexington, found a
pay phone, and called her. It rang for a while, and finally she
answered. She was fine, and very apologetic in her overly polite
way. She must have been in the back bedroom when the doorbell
rang, she said, and it took her a while to get to the phone. She'd
become much slower since I'd last seen her, she told me. I had a
sudden picture of her all alone in that big old house; her life was
harder than I'd thought. In fact, I hadn't really thought much
about her life at all until then, and for the second time that
morning, I felt put in my place.

The year before, 1975, my grandmother had lost both
her son (my uncle) and her husband, my father's stepfa-
ther—"granddaddy" to me. (He used to joke about all the d's in
this appellation, and added extra ones when he signed cards to
me.) As I write this now, having lost my wife and my father in the
last year, within a month of each other, I can understand a little
better what my grandmother was going through at the time. But
even now there are distances of suffering that separate us. I was
50 in my cataclysmic year of loss; she was 80. There is a difference between being in the middle of your life (or not far past the
middle) when the floor drops out of it, and being near the end.
Her devastation was suffered in old age—in the abandonment,
debility, vulnerability, and loneliness of old age: specters that, at
51, are undeniably looming up ahead of me on the horizon; but
they are still only on the horizon. For my grandmother, these
specters were in her bedroom. She slept with them every night.
Not surprising that she hadn't heard the doorbell.

I got just a glimpse of these things before I hung up the pay
phone. And while I cannot say, with Wordsworth—writing of
the death of his father—that it "corrected my desires," my brief
glimpse of her unspeakable loneliness put those desires against
a different background—a different "horizon of expectation." A
horizon of no more expectations, when (or if, as it still seemed
to me then) I ever got to be old. Not a horizon you want to look
for; it was enough to know it was there.

ᡦ

111 E. 64th Street had always been a part of my life. My father had lived there in his high school and college years, and for a while after the war. My parents stayed there after they got married. But when she got pregnant with me, my mother announced that they had to find their own place. She later said, not even half-jokingly, she was afraid that if they didn't get out before I was born, they might never get out. She had a point. My uncle never did. He lived there all his adult life, except for a brief experiment in an apartment on Lexington he named "The Shark" because of the nautical motif he devised for it. He died in his bed at 111, at the age of 58. (This was the bed I slept in my first six months in New York.)

Although we moved to L.A. in 1955, when I was a year old, we returned to New York for a year in 1958, and after that my grandmother's house became our stopping-place for trips abroad and back all through the 60s, in the heyday of my father's work as a screenwriter. I was staying at my grandparents when the Beatles hit the city in February of '64. I got so excited I came down with strep throat—at least that's how the sequence presented itself to me at the time. While I was sick, my uncle went to a Woolworth's on Lexington and bought me *Meet the Beatles*, which I played over and over on my grandparents' portable phonograph in the living room, fantasizing about how I was going to devise a way to do what the title said. They were staying only a few blocks away, at the Plaza.

Later, when I was at Exeter, I stayed at 111 during visits to New York, and then again in college. So my arrival in October of 1976 was by no means a new one. I had a place to call home that I had known all my life.

Unsurprisingly, this was a source of guilt for me—having a family pied-a-terre not only in Manhattan, but on the Upper East Side of Manhattan. The guilt came from knowing that the way had already been paved for me by happenstance of birth, through no doing of my own; and that therefore my experience of "arriving in New York" was somehow invalidated, disqualified from the start, because things had already been comfortably set up for me. I would not have to struggle, I would not have to pay my dues—I would not get to have any of those "authentic" experiences that a genuine newcomer to the city would have had.

I know these ideas may seem ridiculous to some. As Wallace Shawn says in *My Dinner with Andre*, in response to one of Andre's metaphysical flights, "reality is uniform." Meaning that the everyday reality of the cigar shop on the corner, if you were to come to know it fully, is not less valid, worthy, or "deep" than the reality experienced in the spiritual community of Findhorn that Andre has been going on about. In my case, the reality of the "poor little rich boy" (or the person who perceived himself that way, since according to my parents we were not rich; the guilt I felt arose more from the sense of privilege and inequality than from the visible superfluities of wealth) was not inferior, in terms of "authenticity," to the child of poverty, or the struggling youth, or the young man getting off the bus from Duluth, Minnesota. (Or Hibbing.)

I know all this, and I even knew it then, but I did not really believe it, and I still don't. I believe, rather, that my experience is, as the deconstructionists would say, "always already" deauthenticated, sapped of primal energy, disqualified from being "genuine," if only by virtue of being mine, and because of the taint of my own consciousness, and self-consciousness. (This relates to the feeling of a "failed childhood" described in Chapter 2.)

Maybe it all goes back to a primal scene of guilt. (Not the one you're thinking.) In '64 or '65, we were on our way from 111 to the airport, via Harlem and the Triboro Bridge. We were riding in a limo. Why we were doing this I don't recall, since limos weren't really our style. We had always taken taxis to the airport before. But for some reason, this time we were taking a limo. I remember not being at all happy about it, since limos were for rich people, and I already had enough on my (silver) plate without having to worry about being driven around in a limo. I tried to slouch down in my seat so as not to be seen. (My mother, of course, knew exactly what I was up to.)

But it didn't work. As the limo was stopped at a light in Harlem, I saw a black girl about my age (nine or ten) standing on the corner. Our eyes met for a second, and locked. Then she made a back-and-forth, "you and me" gesture with her hands. Her meaning couldn't have been clearer to me: "Let's you and me change places, OK?" or "How about I get some of what you got?" I wanted to slouch back down in my seat again, but that wasn't possible now that she had seen me; I understood such an attempt would have been cowardly, so instead I pretended not to notice. Perhaps it was the girl I was pretending not to notice—even though we had just locked eyes—but more likely it was her gesture. Yet I knew I was deceiving myself: I had noticed and understood everything about our brief exchange. It seemed to take forever for the light to turn.

As far as I am concerned, it still hasn't. In a way, I am still back inside that limo, looking at that girl on the Harlem street-corner, who is looking back at me, getting the whole picture in an instant, and making the "you and me" gesture, which I am still pretending, unsuccessfully, not to notice.

For the nearly four years I lived in New York after college, 111 E. 64th Street was my home base. I stayed in various other places in Manhattan—mostly sublets from friends on the Upper West Side, in Inwood (at the northern tip of the island), and in the West Village—but never for more than eight months at a time. My work situation was much the same.

I had come to New York hoping to get a job in publishing. I had an interview with the editor-in-chief of Doubleday a couple of days after my arrival. The interview had been set up by an old friend of my father's, Billy Abrahams—himself a distinguished editor and biographer. The interview itself went well, I thought. (But what did I know? The only other job interview I'd had was for a brief stint as a security guard.) Unfortunately for me, however, the job application process at Doubleday's included taking a typing test. Factoring in all the mistakes I made, I clocked in at 12 words per minute. It was clear that I wasn't going to qualify for even an entry-level position until my typing improved, so I bought a typing manual and focused on that for the next couple of weeks. My second typing test showed some improvement—20 w.p.m. But Doubleday wasn't impressed, and they didn't ask me back a third time. At the beginning of December I went to work as a reservations clerk at a squash club that had just opened up on E. 86th Street. My other jobs there included sales clerk and racket-stringer in the pro shop, pro shop manager (a disaster: I never once succeeded in balancing the cash register), bartender, and short-order cook.

From the kitchen of the squash club I went on to work in a northern-Italian "family-style" restaurant, owned and run by the chef, a reactionary Serb, who demoted me from waiter to busboy my first night on the job, when I proved incapable of cutting deals with the customers regarding what "family-style" meals he was willing to serve them. For some reason, he refused to serve veal after 9 p.m., but would reconsider if they were willing to order an expensive wine.

That first night, a foursome with a reservation came in at nine and ordered veal marsala. When I went to the kitchen to place the order, Peter snapped back, "No veal after 9 p.m. House rules. Tell them they can have chicken marsala. Go!"

I went and told them (with a slight rephrasing) what he said. One of the women replied, "Listen. I made this reservation a week ago. I spoke to Peter, and told him we would be ordering veal. So you just go back and tell him we would like what we ordered, please."

I went back. "Peter, table one says they ordered veal a week ago when they made their reservation. They say they talked to you."

From the range where he was flipping and stirring he quickly took two long strides to the half-door that separated the kitchen from the alcove where we picked up the orders and bussed the dishes. He glared at me over the door. His wide-spaced gray eyes were baleful, his eyebrows were flecked with Alfredo sauce, and his lower lip jutted out from under his virtually nonexistent upper lip, in an expression I came to know all too well as his "on-the-rampage" look.

"No! Unacceptable!" he snarled. "You are siding with them. Never side with the customers. We are at war with them. The customer is the enemy. That's Rule Number One. Rule Number Two: No veal after 9 p.m. No exceptions."

"But they said—"

"No! You don't understand. I don't care what they said. They are liars. Either they made an earlier reservation or they did not ask for veal. End of discussion. Finalize their order. Go!"

"Look boss," said Ziggy, the Macedonian dishwasher and dessert-server, pointing to a piece of paper stuck to the wall of the kitchen. "It say here veal marsala, 9 p.m."

Peter wheeled around and glared at the slip of paper, as though it, not the dishwasher, had spoken, while Ziggy, behind him, smiled at me and winked. I felt profoundly grateful to him. That would later change, after he almost kicked me in the nuts when I forgot we were out of mocha torte and tried to order some. But for now, we were allies against the terror and injustice of Greater Serbia.

Back at the range, Peter said to me, in a slightly milder voice, "You need to learn how to negotiate. Tell them they can have the veal if they order the Brunello di Montalcino. Go!" The Brunello, at $75 a bottle, was the most expensive wine on the menu (this was 1979).

I didn't have a good feeling about this, but I went back to the table and relayed the message. The woman who had spoken before now put on her sweetest smile and said, "Well you just go tell Peter to stick it up his ass. We're leaving, and we're never coming back."

"Liberal Democrats," was Peter's response. "We didn't want them anyway."

He let me know, in no uncertain terms, that it was my fault that they'd walked; I'd "blown the deal." That was my first and last night as a waiter. I clearly did not possess the negotiating skills needed for the job. At the end of the evening, he told me I was being "demoted" to busboy. But that was fine with me. Not only was it a more lowly and humiliating job (which somewhat—but only somewhat—allayed my ongoing sense of guilt for living at 111 E. 64th St.), it was also much lower-pressure than being a waiter, and actually kind of fun. The only orders I had to keep track of were desserts and coffee (included in the price of the "family-style" dinner), and there was no negotiating involved. I could serve and observe the customers without having to haggle with them. I left that up to Dan and Milano.

Milano was a cousin of Peter's, though they didn't resemble each other at all. Milano was not nearly as fierce-looking, and distinctly Transylvanian in appearance, with dark, slicked-back, obviously dyed hair, bushy eyebrows (also dyed?), a fleshy, hooked nose, and what I suppose would be called a "sensuous" mouth.

At least, that was what I was worried it was. Milano had a way of coming up to me when it was not busy and "engaging" me in conversation by putting his face about two inches from mine, and posing weird, suggestive questions in a singsongy voice, like "Did you have a bath today?"

"I don't take baths, Milano."

"I see," he smiled. "Well then, did you have a shower today?"

"Yes, Milano."

"And was it good?"

"It was adequate."

"Adequate! Aha, ahahaha!" And he would break into giggles,

not taking his face from mine. It was always up to me to remove myself from his proximity; or, if I was lucky, Peter would call him from the kitchen, and then he would start, and make a characteristic little hopping motion as he hurried off, reflexively smoothing down the sides of his already slicked-back hair with his palms.

What made me uneasy about Milano was not that he was probably gay, or at any rate bi (that was the least of his problems, as far as I was concerned), but that he was almost certainly demented. I did my best never to be alone with him in the cellar, where the changing lockers were located. He would arrive in the late afternoon from Astoria with his shirt unbuttoned to the navel, showing a forest of chest hair, with gold chains enmeshed in it like vines. This lush undergrowth would then be covered by his white work shirt and black clip-on bow tie (I was the only one who wore a real bow tie—a matter of pride with me, going back to my Classics days at Exeter)—only to sprout out again at the end of the evening, when he returned to Astoria.

"Would you like to come for a ride in my new van?" he tried to tempt me one night, the dracular mouth within striking range of my neck. "It is very nice. It is, aha, a *love van*."

"I'm sure it is, Milano. But not tonight, thanks."

"Some other night, then?"

"I don't think so, Milano."

"Or any other night? Or every other night? Or every night? Or all night long? Is that the way, aha, aha, you like it?" he sang, gyrating his flabby hips.

I stepped back—way back—and he disappeared into the night, home to his castle in Astoria.

Dan and I had some good laughs over Milano and his antics. Though Dan, as his partner most nights (on the job I mean!), dealt with him in a different and often less amusing capacity. Milano didn't put his face into Dan's. Instead, he would sometimes screw up orders and get caught in the pincer movement of the customer's displeasure on one side and Peter's glaring, lower-lip-jutting wrath on the other—which, as already indicated, could take a sadistic turn.

"Milano, I'm gonna have to fire you, and then it's back to Belgrade, buddy," Peter laughed. "Or maybe you can stay here and go on welfare." (Which in his book was even worse.) "Then you won't be mooching off me anymore—you can go mooch off the Democrats!"

Looking rather crestfallen, Milano smoothed down the sides of his hair and hopped out of the alcove, keeping his distance for a while. I felt kind of sorry for him. Dan whispered, out of the corner of his mouth (as was his way), "Milano has been *duly reprimanded*." Then he threw his head up and to the side and laughed (another characteristic gesture), displaying crooked, sometimes wine-stained teeth, and even less of a chin than I have. I was aware of a sense of superiority over him, even as I disapproved of it. To harbor such feelings was a dubious and cheap comfort; besides, it constituted a sort of betrayal, since I recognized in Dan another "figure of failure," one of a series in my life, going back to Paul and Frank. These figures were to be respected as much as pitied. According to the Hildegarde Gidding, lapsed-Catholic scheme of things, they were examples of innocence, purity, even a kind of nobility of soul, and also sources of instruction in those same virtues—as well as teachers of a more cautionary tale: There but for the grace of God go I. There was an inevitably condescending quality to one's attitude toward "figures of failure"; hence my feeling of superiority to Dan. Hence also the hypocrisy at the core of the whole "enterprise of failure." For at the same time that I could hold up failure as something not to be despised (as most people did), I also rejected failure as an example for myself, and was even terrified lest the example rub off on me. I was always careful to put sufficient distance between the sympathy with which I regarded a "figure of failure" and the figure himself. (Yet my awareness of my hypocrisy in adopting such a two-pronged approach was somehow not sufficient to banish it from practice. One could feel sympathetic towards the "figure of failure" and, at the same time, desirous to avoid his fate.)

But it would be unfair to see Dan McDonald as just a "figure of failure." He was an interesting, intelligent, educated man who—like so many single people who have made their home in New York—was a bit of a loner and an oddball. He came originally from Natchez, Mississippi, and his southern roots showed themselves not only in his accent—not a strong one, since he'd been living in New York for years—but also in his syntax and vocabulary: "might could," "right quick," and "the hutch" to refer to the breakfront in the dining room where we kept the silverware, napkins, glasses, and bags of bread. He'd been a waiter for a while, but before that he'd worked for years in fundraising, including at Tulane University. As part of that job he'd traveled all around the south, often by train, and had stories of the old dining cars that were still in existence, even into the 60s. He loved classical music, and had recently begun to take piano lessons. (Vladimir Horowitz lived right around the corner from the restaurant, and a few times we spotted him walking past the window. One time he even came in to inquire about what sort of fish we were serving. Apparently it wasn't the right kind.) Dan was something of a music snob, and looked down on everything but classical music and traditional jazz. In fact, he was a bit of a cultural snob in general, and had a way of dismissing books, movies, plays, and also food and clothing, that somehow fell below his unspecified but exacting standards. He would declare, sniffily, "I don't go in myself for *that sort of thing*." Although I knew that these opinionated judgments were not to be taken all that seriously, they nevertheless made me feel that my own enthusiasms—not exactly philistine them-selves—were jejune compared to Dan's. I think this may have been part of a half-conscious strategy, despite our genuine liking for one another, to put me in my place—not just as his junior (by some 20 years at least), and as the busboy, but also as a cultural amateur.

Part of what made Dan a successful waiter (read: negotiator) was the glass of red wine he kept behind the cappuccino machine on busy nights, and which lubricated his passage between the Peter–customer pincers' movement that Milano tended to get caught in. His years as a fundraiser helped him to sell people on the "family-style" dining concept, and to conceal from them the fact that they were, essentially, powerless enemy pawns in Peter's hostile gastronomic campaign. Should they ever make the mistake of wanting veal after 9 p.m., Dan had a way of either disabusing them of this conceit, or making them pay dearly for it by ordering the Brunello. Where Milano was a bundle of tension and fear in the negotiation process, a deer caught in the opposing oncoming headlights of Peter and the diners, Dan was all smoothness and Southern laughter, flowing like wine.

He kept himself to one or two glasses on the weekends, though sometimes after work we would go out for a beer and burger at the Madison Pub. We would share war stories. He would tell me about his former life down South, and his musical interests, and I would hear about "The Other McDonald's", the gracious, Southern-style restaurant he fantasized about opening someday in New York, where the customers were always right, could order anything they wanted, and where Democrats and homosexuals were welcome (the latter two, under Peter's regime, being not only proscribed, but synonymous).

I don't think Dan was gay. From time to time he would mention girlfriends he'd had, but he'd never married, and seemed to have settled into a confirmed bachelorhood. He had an apartment in a rent-controlled building in Murray Hill where he'd been for a while, another lunchtime job at a high-end bar and grill in midtown, and had recently purchased an upright piano. He'd finally arranged his life just the way he wanted it, he told me with a hint of self-satisfaction: beholden to no one, free and independent in the capital of the world. To me, of course, there was a note of sadness in his well-arranged life. Was he lonely? My mother would have seen him that way—a Father MacKenzie figure ("Eleanor Rigby" was another anthem in her Greatest Hits of Pathos, right up there with "Nowhere Man")—and so, not surprisingly, I couldn't help seeing him that way too, while at the same time remaining conscious that I was projecting our distorted imaginings onto him. There were certainly other ways—less romanticized and condescending, more realistic and common-sensical ways—of seeing him than merely as a "figure of failure." Why should the idea of failure—anyone's failure, for that matter—override other ways of looking at a person?

The question goes to the heart of the whole "figure of failure" syndrome (a syndrome—indeed, a kind of illness—of the perceiver much more than the object of perception). I am reminded of a short story in the *New Yorker*, which my mother brought to my attention, years ago. I still remember the title, though not much else; it was called "The Soft Core." I seem to recall it was about a parent and child. Son and mother? That probably would have been too obvious. Daughter and father? Maybe—my mother had been very close to her own father. I believe the title referred to the "soft core" of vulnerability in all of us, as perceived by the son or daughter. My mother wordlessly handed me the story to read, I read it, and duly took its point.

This little incident may help to explain my mother's privileging of, or even attraction to, the "failure factor" in human experience. Success is hard, in all senses: It is difficult to achieve; it has a hard surface—and core as well—in that it toughens you in the process of acquiring it, making you both tougher on yourself and on others. Failure, on the other hand, represents "the soft core" referred to in the *New Yorker* story: those who are softer, more vulnerable, weaker by nature, who lack the hardness and toughness to achieve success in the unforgiving world. Or, if by some chance they do experience success, are nevertheless unable to hold onto it. Those of us who value the "soft core"—the mushy, the sentimental, the romantic, the dreamy, the vulnerable, the weak—will also tend to value failure, which resides in "the soft core," and emanates from it.

In any case, whatever Dan may be doing today, I like to think of him as owner and host of "The Other McDonald's," presiding over a tolerant and cultured establishment of fine food and music, with classical and traditional jazz tunes playing in the daytime, and, in the evenings, featuring the piano artistry of the proprietor himself.

Though I had various jobs and residences in my time in New York, there was one goal I pursued consistently during those four years: I wanted to be a writer. To my mind, this desire was actually validated by my failure to get a job in publishing. Working in publishing, I now came to believe, was incompatible with the creative inner life necessary for a writer, whereas working as a sales clerk, cook, and busboy was not: the idea being that in menial jobs, your mind is your own, whereas in "professional" jobs, your mind is somehow "invaded" and "co-opted" by the work you do. Not an original idea (or a true one), but it possessed for me, at the time, a ring of truth all the more convincing because it seemed to confirm the "rightness" of my failure even to get my foot in the door of the publishing business. My friend Howard, on the other hand, held that "nothing corrupts"; that you were going to do what you really wanted to do, regardless (or because) of the obstacles (e.g., Joseph Heller in advertising; Wallace Stevens and Kafka as insurance lawyers; Hemingway as a journalist, etc.). While this seemed true—as did just about everything Howard said about art, people, and the way the world worked; his was the crucial friendship in my life—and I wanted very much to believe it, I didn't really. Maybe this was because, like all romantics, I was an idealist, and Howard was a realist. From my Catholic mother I had absorbed a belief in purity, and therefore corruption. Howard believed in neither.

He was born and raised a Jew, and had a more secure identity, both Jewish and otherwise, than I did. And because I believed in purity and corruption, at least with regard to the literary life, I believed also that there was something almost providential in my failing the typing test. I was not meant to go into publishing, and by not doing so, I was able to save my creative energy for my own writing, rather than have it be diverted into working on other people's. (This belief was soon enough given the lie in Hollywood, where I became a synopsizer of other writers' scripts and books. And, after that, in academia, where I became a critic of other writers' works.) But I believed it in my New York years, and it was not a bad thing that I did. It was a sustaining belief, a "necessary fiction," that helped me see my series of jobs not only as "paying my dues" and "grist for the mill," but also as a way of preserving and protecting my creative energy and idealism.

The question of corruptibility had come up in connection with something that had been said to me by Isabel Eberstadt, Nick's mom. At lunch one day we had been talking about writing, and she said that it didn't matter what I did, as long as I kept writing, and as long as I stayed out of advertising. (Ironically, Nick had earlier remarked that I should go into advertising. "Why?" I asked. "Because you could make a lot of money," he replied. I remember being hurt by this view of my abilities and motives.) But Isabel now gave me to understand that advertising meant something like death for a writer—hence the discussion with Howard afterwards.

During my first year or two in New York, and especially the first few months, the Eberstadts were an important presence in my life. In the fall of '76, when I arrived in New York, Nick had started graduate school at Harvard, but his parents, whom I had met before, lived ten blocks away from my grandmother's house, on Park Avenue. They invited me out to lunch a few times, and once gave me a ticket to a screening of Eric Rohmer's film *The Marquise von O.* Afterwards I made the faux-pas of telling their daughter Nenna I wished it had had more humor. She replied that she thought it *did* have humor, and was actually very funny, in an understated way. Then I felt like an oaf for not having gotten it, unsophisticated, perhaps even vulgar in my sense of humor, at least in comparison with the Eberstadts, who were to me the quintessence of New York wit and refinement.

Isabel was the daughter of Ogden Nash, and had grown up in Baltimore society. Her father had been friends with S.J. Perelman ("Sid", she called him), which struck a note with me because Perelman was one of my father's favorite writers (the law firm of "White, Lipped, and Trembling" was often quoted by him). Isabel had once visited him in L.A., when he was working there as a screenwriter. She was graciousness and sensitivity personified—a sort of aristocratic version of my mother—and it was part of her exquisite manners to display some familiarity with Hollywood in order to put me more at my ease. Why was this necessary? Perhaps because she sensed my discomfort at the fact that my father was a Hollywood screenwriter, and so not a "serious" writer. (He'd said to me more than once, "If you want to be a writer, be a *real* writer, not a screenwriter," and I had taken him at his word. I sometimes wonder if that wasn't a mistake.) Isabel's refinement of manners and sensibility, like Nenna's comment about the Rohmer movie, made me acutely conscious of how I might fall short in these areas. I remember I once used the word "jerk" to describe someone, and she said, "Josh, I have to tell you, I really don't like that word. Please don't say it again." I was mortified. A word I had given no thought to, and in fact had used countless times, had offended her, and I had not a clue why. My cluelessness only increased my mortification, because it exposed the depths of my ignorance, which also seemed a kind of cultural (and perhaps even moral) failure. It wasn't until some time later, thinking back on this incident, that I realized the reason for her offense: "Jerk", of course, is short for "jerk-off."

Not long after I'd left New York and moved back to L.A., Isabel's novel *Natural Victims* was published. I will admit to having the insane idea that the title may have been suggested by her acquaintance with me, among others—losers, that is. Of course I didn't flatter myself that I was the principal or worst loser she knew. But I figured that in the writing of a novel about parents and children—specifically, about a runaway daughter—it would be natural to make comparisons between one's own children and other people's. By such a reckoning, I would be an example of one of the "natural victims," fear of whom her novel may have been written, in part, to exorcise.

Her husband Fred was dark, sardonic, and witty, sometimes unsparing in his observations of people. (In the last three traits Nick took after him.) I was intimidated by him. He had a cleft in his chin that, coupled with a full moustache, for some reason made him even more intimidating, as though the cleft and the moustache together were the sign of a bunching together of mental strength that was implacable. I once said "neck" when I meant "throat," and he corrected me. The difference had never occurred to me before. I called myself an aspiring writer, and I didn't know the difference between "throat" and "neck"? Of course he never said or even implied this, but in my intimidation I felt it. The correction may have been meant helpfully: There is a difference, and you should know it; precision is one of the main tools of your trade. But it rattled me nonetheless, just as Nenna's demurral and Isabel's exception to the word "jerk" had rattled me. In the presence of the Eberstadts, my seeming short-comings of brains and background were constantly before me. My problem, no doubt, and of my own making. Just one of the prices to be paid, I reminded myself (and not without a measure of self-congratulation mixed in with the self-denigration), for a growing acquaintance with New York sophistication.

My mother, who somewhat abashedly subscribed to *W Weekly*, would get a kick out of seeing the Eberstadts in its pages on a regular basis, and from this she concluded that they were "jet-setters," or "beautiful people." I rejected these labels, because they seemed inadequate to convey the reality of the Eberstadts' fascination and idiosyncratic style, as I had come to know them. They were much too smart, ironic, and tasteful to be encompassed by those terms, which seemed to apply rather to the ostentatiously wealthy, and those who put looks before brains.

Though they certainly were wealthy. Fred's father Ferdinand, a prominent Wall Street lawyer and investment banker, had founded F. Eberstadt & Co. During World War II, as vice chairman of the War Production Board, he masterminded the production and control of strategic materials. He also helped to create the National Security Council and the U.N. Atomic Energy Commission. His biography, unsurprisingly (and in contrast to the Gidding tradition), is entitled *The Will to Win*. Nick said it was his grandfather he modeled himself after.

Nenna, Nick's younger sister, was named after Ferdinand, her full name being "Fernanda," another example of the unique Eberstadtian style. She had a milder version of the upturned Eberstadt nose (actually, it came from her mother's side, but to me it was always the "Eberstadt nose"), and large eyes that took in everything, widening with interest at news of some noteworthy perversity or strangeness, for which she, like her brother, had a seemingly insatiable appetite. This mannerism may have been taken from William F. Buckley, a friend of the family, along with some of Buckley's speech patterns. When she was in high school (which was when I knew her), Nenna had an upper-crust, British-sounding accent. It was especially apparent on the phone. While I recognized this as a teenage affectation, to me it was intriguing and exciting, one more inflection of the Eberstadtian mystique. (Maybe it was also her way of getting ready for college. She went to Magdalen, at Oxford—where she got a First, of course. Was there nothing these Eberstadts couldn't do? No world-oyster they couldn't shuck?) But while Nenna's accent, back then, was the most pronounced, they all had a unique way of speaking, with individual variations (the parents, following the parlance of high society, softened their r's; Nick's speech was blunt and direct), but sharing some common features: witty, refined, urbane, allusive without being pedantic. They used certain slang phrases with relish: "ground to a halt," "the runt of the litter," "a Dr. Feelgood." But there was also about their formulations an element of surgical objectivity, even of cruelty, of which I was at least once the object.

Nenna is now a successful writer, with four novels, a nonfiction book about gypsies, and many articles and reviews to her credit. I remember Nick showing me an early story she had written, about inviting a boy over for dinner to meet her family. The story was funny and well written, but that wasn't what interested me. What interested me was the look it provided into the family, through the eyes of one of its members. After reading it I said something lame like "Nenna's really great," at which Nick immediately shot back, "Yeah, and you're not going to marry her." I was stunned. But rather than fighting back, or resisting such a cynical construction of my motives (like the advertising comment earlier), I assumed it must be true because it was coming from Nick, who could basically do no wrong in my eyes. After all, my comment had sounded a bit obsequious; maybe there was something else under that obsequiousness that I hadn't even been aware of until Nick's sucker-punch knocked it out of me. Natural victims allow themselves to get beaten up; sometimes they even ask for it.

And, to be honest, his comeback was not without some truth to it—which was part of the reason it stung. He had intuited that I had been allowing myself to fantasize, however vaguely, about marrying Nenna, and thus entering the charmed world of the Eberstadts on an intimate and permanent basis. Not that this was a scenario I spent a lot of time on. Furthermore, my fantasies regarding the Eberstadts were never really entertained seriously, or unselfconsciously. They were themselves the result of another fantasy, this one even crazier and (now) more embarrassing: the fantasy of myself as an American Proust. Having read all seven volumes of *Remembrance of Things Past* in a course my senior year in college, I was still very much under its sway. (And still am, and probably always will be—another proof of my literary minordom, my Bloomian "weakness", as well as what I feel to be my failure to be Proust. Sad—and insane—but true.) At the time, I was seeing much of my experience through Proustian eyes, and according to such a vision, the Eberstadts were my Guermantes. Coming to know them nourished a hope in me that perhaps, just perhaps, I had a destiny not unlike Proust's. This delusion may seem a bit less insane when I add that the effect of immersing myself in all of *Remembrance* during those rapturous ten weeks of senior year at Berkeley was not so much to make me think that someday I might be the American Proust, as simply to encourage me to believe that my life was important, and that it could be written about (under cover of fiction, as I wanted to write about it then) in such a way as to make it seem important to others, too. Reading Proust provided me with hope of a specifically autobiographical nature, of which this project is the strange fruit.

But there came a time, at the end of my four years in New York, when I ran out of creative energy. I had recently finished a manuscript for a novella that had been rejected by the same publisher who was about to publish my first novel. The sense of success I might otherwise have felt at the prospect of publication was therefore canceled out in advance by the knowledge of my subsequent failure. A zero-sum game of sorts. Enough to take the wind out of anyone's sails. Still, I was about to have my first novel published. You'd think I would have been able to get at least a little pleasure out of that—out of the thought of it, the pride of the accomplishment, the anticipation of actually holding the book in my hands. And I did. But, in a kind of reversal of the "sustaining belief" mentioned earlier, the thought of even the near future, when I would be what I thought I had most wanted to be, "a published novelist," now seemed a feeble thing in comparison to the barren-feeling present, where I was in the process of being dumped by my girlfriend, had had my novella rejected, was unemployed, and was living once more at grandma's. What now? My soon-to-be-ex had said that jobs in New York were plentiful, and easy to get if you were willing to work. Sympathy wasn't her strong suit, but her hard-nosed realism did cause me to wonder: Wasn't I willing to work? After all, in the past four years I had written a novel and a novella, a bunch of short stories (unpublished), and had also held several jobs at the squash club and the restaurant. Surely they would hire me back in some capacity, or I could get a job somewhere else. My girlfriend was right: There were lots of jobs out there, especially restaurant jobs that kept your mind free to write. The problem was, now I didn't want to have my mind free to write, because I had nothing to write. I was all written out. I didn't want another job in New York, and my girlfriend didn't want me. I wanted to go home. And so I did. I had failed to make it in New York.

But just what did that mean? What had I wanted to do? What would have defined "success" for me? Had I even given any thought to the matter? I had no plan, no clear objectives, no measure of success. I had thought I wanted to "go into publishing," but after failing the typing test the second time I gave up on that, and went to work in the squash club. At the time, this hadn't seemed like such a failure. Sure, my wretched typing skills were an embarrassment—but, as I said, I saw this as confirmation of my creative destiny, rather than my professional doom. My future success as a writer (what kind of success and what kind of writer I hadn't bothered to ask myself) would vindicate my humiliation at Doubleday. Besides, working at the squash club, where there were lots of employees in their 20s like myself, was fun. I had a summer romance with a girl who worked with me in the pro shop, before she went off to college. I played squash several times a week, for free. Working at Peter's restaurant was mostly fun, too. I had another romance with one of the waitresses there, Liz Secord, a sweet young woman from Ohio, who was studying to be a nurse. This time it was me who dumped her, after she came back from a short vacation in the Berkshires—the first time I'd dumped anyone. Why? Maybe because she was too nice to me; or because I sensed she was getting ready to settle down, and that frightened me, and threatened the vision of the solitary, striving writer I had concocted in my lonely imagination. Satisfaction, settlement, middle-class family life were creative death, I thought.

Or maybe it was really the idea of New York, of myself there, that I was in love with during those four years, and this idea didn't leave room for anyone else. The New York that all young people who move there fall in love with, because it reflects back to them their own excitement, energy and great expectations. It was not really a career I wanted at all. I came to understand this clearly after flunking the typing test. It was New York itself I was after. It was life, love, the daily, hourly, minute-by-minute exhilaration of simply being alive, which the cornucopia of New York pours forth to the dazzled young guests at the feast.

And for once, self-consciousness did not spoil my enjoyment. It may even have enhanced it. To walk down the street was to have an experience—a "New York experience." Because I was not just walking down the street; I was walking down the street *in New York*. Even more, I was doing this as a resident of New York. I lived there now. I was becoming familiar with the city, making it my own—as countless other young people had done before me. But that didn't matter. In fact, the proverbial, mythical pattern of my "New York experience" only seemed to further enhance and validate its meaning. Because my experience was a time-worn, American rite of passage, I thought that it could not fail to have an edifying effect on me, forming a necessary stage in my development as a writer.

The constant daily stimuli of life in New York brought me out of myself; and the constant walking I did was the perfect kind of exercise—moderate and prolonged—to keep my thoughts from becoming too brooding. Walking helped to energize my imagination, and to give it an expansive rather than depressive cast (which it tends to have otherwise). Walking in New York also helped me check that imagination with a dose of reality: the solid presence of old buildings, and people of all sorts—an endless variety of New Yorkers on their rounds of business and pleasure. Those for whom the best was yet to come (I at the time among them, despite what I might have thought then); those in the middle of the best (what I call the "Major Period" of one's life); and those whose best days were behind them, who were now living out their "Minor Period" (I again among them, now). The beginning, middle, and end of the journey; and New York one of the great world crossroads of this journey.

It was only in the last few weeks before I left New York, in June of 1980, that I began to see my years living there as a failure. It wasn't that I had failed at anything in particular. The blown opportunity at Doubleday had stopped bothering me as soon as I got the job at the squash club. It was enough to be working in New York. I didn't care, at that stage, what work I did. And I can't even say that my failure to get the novella published was either a surprise or a crushing disappointment. I knew it was seriously flawed, and that writing it had been a kind of self-indulgent busy work, rather than something my heart was in. Given that my underlying purpose in coming to New York had really just been to live there, work there, and write there, couldn't I claim success in all three of these endeavors? Furthermore, not only had I written in New York, I had written a novel, which was about to be published. How was it possible to snatch defeat from the jaws of this small but real victory? How was I able to turn this record of modest success into a feeling of failure?

Because I was running away, and I knew it. I was running away from my small success. Perhaps because it was a small success, and not something larger and grander—though I didn't know that then. For all I knew, it could be about to be a large success, or at least a critical success (it was neither). But it wasn't the smallness or the largeness of the success that I was running away from as much as the fact that it was a success of the sort I had most wanted, or had thought I most wanted: the publication of a novel. The recognition that this was about to happen freaked me out. I call it the "hiding-in-the-bathroom syndrome," and it has been a habit of mine since grade school. New York was the school where I was about to take a test, Pacific Palisades was my bathroom, and I took off for its comforting, quiet shelter, where I could mull things over on the toilet for as long as I wanted. And what I most wanted to mull over was how it had come about that I was made so differently from the way I thought I was made. There are some who are just not made to succeed. Not in the sense that they try and try and never succeed (though there are certainly those), but in the sense that as soon as they do succeed, they disown it and run from it. I had begun to recognize that I was one of them.

8

My Failure as a Writer

"Men have oftener suffered from the mockery of a place
too smiling for their reason than from the oppression of
surroundings over-sadly tinged."

Thomas Hardy, *The Return of the Native*

In the spring of 1978 I had gotten an idea for a novel, based on
the character of my grandmother, and wanted to see if I could
write it. At the time I was living with my friends Adam and
Howard in a vast five-bedroom apartment in the BelNord, on
the Upper West Side, that Adam's parents had just vacated. (My
share of the rent was $97 a month. Hard to believe, but true.) I
could have stayed there and continued to work at the squash club
while starting to write the novel, but I didn't want to. I wanted to
write full-time, and the only way I thought I could do that was to
move back to my parents' house in L.A. Besides, I had developed
a crush on Howard's girlfriend Mary, an artist who made paper
dresses and shoes, and then modeled them. Mary was spending
a lot of time in our apartment, and I knew that if I stayed there I
wouldn't get much work done—and might lose my best friend

in the bargain. I felt the time had come to leave New York for a while and see whether I had it in me to write this novel. Perhaps I would go down to Baja and write there—my parents had a small getaway south of Ensenada, overlooking the ocean. No phone, no electricity—just gaslights and refrigerator. The sound of the waves breaking over the rocks below. What better place to start a novel?

As it happened, I did no writing in Baja; I only went down there once that summer, for a few days. But I did a lot of writing in Pacific Palisades. I lived there from May to November, and wrote the first half of the novel. I sent it to Billy Abrahams, my father's old friend who'd gotten me the interview at Doubleday, and who at the time was a senior editor at Holt, Rinehart and Winston. Billy liked it and gave me a contract, and a modest advance. In November I returned to New York, triumphant. Another arrival in New York, very different from two years before, and even more exciting; this time I did feel like a conqueror of sorts, and finished the novel the following June.

So where is the failure? you ask. Sounds like a success story. Guy signs a contract with a major publisher for his first novel. Where's the failure in that? All writers should have such a failure.

No, they shouldn't. They don't—the vast majority don't, anyway—and they shouldn't. That was my first failure as a writer: premature success. It was all too easy, both the writing and the selling. By the writing, I mean the circumstances of the writing: in the bosom of home, with no rent to pay, no living to earn, nowhere to be and nothing to do but write every day. With the southern California sun shining and the ocean only a couple of blocks away—it was wonderful. A memorable summer. I loved it, and I felt—uncharacteristically—that I had earned it. I'd worked at the squash club for a year and a half—not exactly hard labor, but hot and sweaty enough in the kitchen that I could feel virtuous as I rode the 86th St. crosstown bus home in my dirty chef's outfit: black and white checked trousers and white chef's jacket (a present from my father). And a little bit of that proud worker's virtue still remained over the summer as I wrote my novel in easy, too-easy circumstances, surrounded by sunlight and greenery and all the comforts of home.

Of course I loved it. But a little part of me—the boy in the limo—knew there was something wrong with this picture. That it was too happy, too easy—as Hardy writes, "too smiling for my reason." The circumstances of the novel's writing were reflected in its content: light, insubstantial, over-written, precious. Not that I aimed at writing like Bellow, or Kafka, or Mann—three of my literary heroes. (Mann, oddly enough, lived in Pacific Palisades from 1941 to 1952. That the sage of Lübeck, the creator of Hans Castorp and Gustave von Aschenbach and Adrien Leverkühn—*Doctor Faustus* was written entirely in the Palisades!—might have walked on the same bland streets on which I later rode my bike and skateboard is a continual source of amazement to me. I have thought of writing a novel about this, called *Sehnsucht in the Palisades*. Will I ever do this, or will it be just another literary failure of mine? Or will that failure itself be the subject of the story?)

The example of such luminaries was bound to influence my idea of what it was possible for writers to do. And also, what it was *not* possible for them to do: that is, writers such as myself, whose aspirations were too great for their talent, and who could not quite reconcile themselves to this disparity. It seems to me that my talent is such that I should have been content with aiming at less in literary terms: screenwriting, TV writing, thriller or detective or sex–money–power novels. Not that these kinds of writing are easy, either. But I never even tried them. Why not? Arrogance? Snobbery? Over-education? The residual elitism of a classics major (the beneficiary of "Exeter Greek and Latin")? The taking too seriously of lofty literary models? Or, more simply, lack of talent for commercial writing? Inability to tell a story, to come up with a plot line and develop it coherently and credibly? An inability not to go off on tangents, to resist the urge to indulge my tendency to digress? The taking of the example of Proust much too seriously, and personally even? The failure to see that what was possible for Proust is just not possible for me, that he has done it infinitely better than I ever could? (I have actually written an essay entitled "On My Failure to Be Proust" which, of course, has been rejected by a number of journals.)

When *The Old Girl* was published in August of 1980 I was already in a funk; and over the following weeks that funk turned into a depression. The reasons for the depression had partly to do with the novel, and partly with a relationship that had failed (the girlfriend who'd dumped me). My expectations for my first novel were unrealistic. I had thought that being published would somehow transform me—not just from an unpublished writer into a "published novelist," but that it would produce fundamental changes for the better in my status, my livelihood, my romantic life. Whereas it produced changes in none of those things. Byron said that he awoke the morning after publication of *Childe Harold* to "find himself famous." I awoke the morning after publication of *The Old Girl* to find myself exactly the same. What had I expected? A magical transformation? A transubstantiation of my earthly matter into that more refined essence of "author"—an entirely different level of being? Was I such a child, or fantasist, that I actually believed this? Did I expect the offers from magazine editors and *The New York Times Book Review* to come flooding in? Requests for interviews? Spots on talk shows? I guess I did, unrealistic as that might seem.

Unrealistic, because my novel was far—very far—from being a best seller. I believe it sold 3,000 copies. Perhaps it was 6,000. Certainly the figure was not over 6,000. The sales figures were as predicted, Billy told me. If he was disappointed—and how could he not have been?—he kept it from me, and somehow managed to make me feel reassured by this news. Everything had gone according to plan; I had not disappointed. The distribution system of a major publishing house had certain built-in guarantees of minimum sales below which it was not possible to fall, and my book was part of that system. Of course, those guarantees had nothing to do with the merits of my book, and existed independently of them. I knew this, too; it was part of what was making me depressed. My book hadn't sold more than the minimum predicted, because—as was suddenly and plainly clear to me—it just wasn't that good. And there seemed to be ample evidence to back this up. One reviewer had compared it to a "light and insubstantial pastry crust"; another referred sarcastically to the "fine narrator." *People* panned it (in "Picks & Pans"): the reviewer called my observations "forgettable." Not every response was negative; one review said that I wrote with a "melancholy intelligence" (a backhanded compliment that I lapped up, since at 26 I was still of the opinion that literary intelligence had to be melancholy). However, the smattering of positive comments only made the negative ones seem all the more definitive.

But as for experiencing the sense of triumph, or even prideful accomplishment, that I had looked forward to since getting the book contract almost two years before, I was very far from that on publication day, and during the weeks and months that followed. Rather than coming as a confirmation of my talent as a writer, publication reinforced my worst fears: that I was a lightweight, a mere charmer, getting by on my superficial verbal facility, without anything more substantial—any deeper talent—to back it up.

These fears were not groundless. In the year since completing the manuscript of the first novel I had written a novella, which had been rejected by my editor, Billy Abrahams. His decision was correct—I knew that even before he made it, even as I was writing the novella. It was entitled *The Man Who Spent the Night in Disneyland*, and was about just that—a longtime fantasy of mine. As an idea for a story it was eccentric, intriguing, original—all of those qualities on which I prided myself. The problem was, my novella was nothing *but* an idea. No plot to speak of, except for the violator being chased by Disneyland security officers. The only other character for my solitary protagonist to interact with during his long (nay, interminable) night in the Magic Kingdom, besides a dog that attached itself to him, was a "hippie chick" camping out on Tom Sawyer's Island (a last remnant of the days when it had been briefly "occupied" in the late 60s or early 70s. The dog belonged to her.). My protagonist attempted to have sex with her, and failed. That was the extent of the book's human interaction.

What was even worse than this poor excuse for a novella—it was really nothing more than a long and thinly veiled auto-biographical essay on existential alienation, in the guise of a novella—was my bad faith in writing it. Halfway through the process, it had dawned on me that I should scrap what I had done and make this a story about two people spending the night in Disneyland. At least that might give it the breath of human life I knew it was lacking. But although I knew, even as I was writing, that this was what I should do, I didn't do it. I trudged along, undeviating from my original misbegotten plan, perversely committed to a losing proposition, as though the purpose of writing were simply to produce pages, day after day; as though there were something virtuous in sticking to plan, even when it was a bad plan.

Nor did I change my ways once the manuscript was rejected. Billy confirmed many of the same criticisms I had sensed when I was writing. I saw their rightness. But I did nothing about it. By that point, of course, I had lost heart; I was depressed. I was in no shape, creatively or emotionally, to undertake a page-one rewrite. And so my knowledge that I had nothing to "follow up" my first novel with only deepened my funk. Publication now seemed like a fluke, and a terminus, rather than the inauguration of a writing career. The word "fluke," or perhaps it was "freak," was actually used by my ex-girlfriend to describe my being published at such a relatively young age (26).

I remember something else told to me during this period, from a more sympathetic source: my best friend Howard, also an aspiring writer. He said: "You have a mystique; I want a career." I have never forgotten those words. I know that the publication of my novel was difficult for him. Before I had even started writing it, he had two complete novels in manuscript, neither of which had stirred up much interest with publishers. Whereas I had gotten a contract with only half a novel to show. So it was not surprising that his pronouncement was tinged with a little envy (and contempt)—though not so much as to alter its fundamental truth. At the time, however, I remember taking it as a compliment more than a criticism, and feeling contempt, in turn, for his desire for a career (which he has gone on to have, successfully, as a screenwriter and director). I thought a career was a base thing, compared to a mystique. After all, a mystique was inimitable, God-given; virtually anyone could have a career if they were willing to work for it. (I, of course, was not, as evidenced by the way I handled the "Disneyland" rejection.)

But I think it was not just laziness, or even depression, that kept me from rewriting "Disneyland." I think it was something else, something more perverse and inscrutable. After I met Diane, who lifted me out of the depression, not only did I not go back to "Disneyland," I began writing other eccentric, ambitious, and willfully uncommercial manuscripts that had no greater likelihood of success than "Disneyland." I wrote several chapters about a yearning housewife who became involved with a biker; another novella, this one much more autobiographical (at least on the surface) than the "Disneyland" debacle, about a mother and son who travel back to Scranton, PA (my mother's home town) to bury her mother; several unpublishably long (40-plus pages) autobiographical stories about the adventures of a sixth-grade boy and his black superhero alter-ego; and, much later, a full-length novel manuscript that combined all of the above—and then some. These efforts were written in the same creative state of mind as "Disneyland," which can best be described as "gush"—a state in which process is everything, and the final product an afterthought. In "gush," editing is seen as an interruption of the sacrosanct creative process, and put off to some vaguely imagined future day in which my creative productivity is on the wane. But that day never comes; I make sure of that. When one gushing fountain stops because it inevitably runs out of water, I simply start another.

I am ashamed to admit all this, not only because as a writer I should know better, but because, as a teacher of writing, I actually do know better. At least where my students' writing is concerned, I know better. I tell them that "writing is rewriting," and I require them to attend several tutorials over the course of the semester, where I go over their writing in detail, and discuss exactly what needs to be rewritten, and how. But I don't practice what I preach. I mentioned above that my failure to seriously rewrite anything I have written, since the publication of my novel over 25 years ago, was more than just laziness or depression. It was something more "perverse" and "inscrutable," though not so inscrutable that I cannot name it: the fear of success. It is the fear of success that keeps me from rewriting. Because if I rewrote—I mean, if I rewrote seriously, with application, with the unswerving mindset and dedication of a serious craftsman—I would be in danger of having my writing be a success. And I am scared of my writing being a success.

Why? Perhaps because then I would have to produce another success, and might come up short, as I did when my first novel was published, and I had nothing to follow it up with. But it is more than that, I think. My fear of success when the novel was published was not just fear of blowing the follow-up; it was fear of the first novel being a success in itself. Fear of attention being focused on me, fear of the limelight, of being exposed as a fraud, a lightweight, a piece of puff pastry (as the review said). How would I deal with success, if it came to me? Would I accept it, however modest it was, and move on from there? Or would I get spooked by success, and run away from it, and drop out of sight? I chose the latter, like the time, in fifth grade at Tocaloma Boys' Club, when I received the much coveted red Sportsmanship Jacket, given at the end of the year to the boy who was not necessarily the best athlete (which I wasn't) but who exemplified "good sportsmanship." I found the whole experience very difficult, not just because of my characteristic self-consciousness, but also because this mark of success made me feel suddenly unworthy. I was on the point of calling up the head of the club, "Robbie" Robinson, to tell him that I really didn't deserve the jacket. I thought about this for several days and discussed it with my parents. They thought I was nuts—especially my mother, who usually understood me so well—and persuaded me that it would be very insulting and ungrateful of me to say anything to Robbie, or to any of the other counselors at Tocaloma. So I desisted in my crazy scheme—but that didn't change my feelings. My mother spent several nights sewing various merit badges onto my Sportsmanship Jacket, but the following year—my last at Tocaloma—I never once wore it. Previously, I had looked on boys who wore the jacket with something like awe, or at least a distanced respect, but the fact that I had now received it seemed thereby to invalidate it (the Groucho Marx syndrome—I wouldn't wear any prize jacket that would have me as its wearer), and even to lower the judgment of Robbie Robinson a little in my eyes. I felt embarrassed and sorry for him. Couldn't he see that to award me the jacket was a sham, a travesty?

The acknowledgment of success also requires a certain emotional maturity, which I lack, as well as a certain renunciation that I seem to be incapable of: the renunciation of my adolescent naiveté in favor of a grown-up sense of reality, a more realistic assessment of my strengths and weaknesses, and what they mean for my possibilities in the world. This failure to renounce my comforting adolescent imaginings is probably connected with the life of privilege that I have led. Dreams die harder when you grow up in candy-ass Pacific Palisades and go to private schools—when you have no harsh, formative, disciplining realities to force you to discard your illusions, to align your sense of what is and is not possible for you with the rigors of the world.

But why do I equate my young imaginings with illusions? Couldn't they just as well be seen as "sustaining beliefs"? Why not call my naiveté "idealism" rather than "illusion"? The imagination is also formative, is it not? I remember once seeing a billboard on a railroad overpass in Worcester, MA. It was a quote from George Eliot: "It is never too late to be what we might have been." I found this quote not only inspiring but reassuring—encouragement, from an unimpeachable source of wisdom, for me to feel vindicated in continuing to retain my high ideals, to indulge my impractical imaginings, which were suddenly—by the agency of that serendipitous billboard and its message—taken out of the realm of mind alone, and brought into the world of the living.

Another thing I liked about the billboard, and which was surely on the mind of whoever had caused it to be placed there, was that it was located in a particularly blighted section of formerly-industrial downtown Worcester, next to abandoned brick factory buildings, and weed-grown culverts, and empty lots. These sad things stirred my imagination, too, though in a very different way from the Eliot quote. (The story of Worcester's place in my life, and its profound appeal to me, is for another time; though that appeal probably also has much to do with my romanticization of failure.)

Fear of success and romanticization of failure—together they combined to ensure that, at the time my novel was published, I would run from success and pursue failure. Furthermore, the perceived high-mindedness of failure—the recognition of high ideals not reached, but still cherished—allowed me to congratulate myself on retaining the purity of my values, rather than compromising them by pursuing success. And so I actually set up failure as a goal to be achieved. I pursued it out of an intuitive realization, like the boy hiding in the bathroom, that I was not equipped—psychologically, organizationally, emotionally—to deal with success. That intuition was covered over with an appearance of noble integrity: It was better to be a loser than a winner. Underneath this perverse romance was the wish to remain a child. The fear of success, the embrace of failure, were variations of the refusal to grow up. "Were"? Still are. A father, and now a widower, and still afraid, at almost 53, of becoming a man.

Those days, weeks, and months after the publication of my novel in 1980 were the worst of my life up till then. I awoke every morning with a grinding dread in my stomach, and over the course of the day the feeling never really left. Nights were better (unlike the experience of many who suffer from depression), and I don't remember having trouble sleeping. Waking was my problem. The light of morning—the pale, waning light of September, October, November in southern California—brought with it a weight of unhappiness I could not fathom. Here I was, a published novelist—that thing I had thought I wanted to be more than anything else. Why was I feeling this way? Then I remembered: I had to get through the coming day, and I didn't see how I could. Though I did know enough, after the first few weeks of persistent dread, to seek out a shrink, who identified my feeling as "free-floating anxiety." It helped a little to put a name to it. The naming seemed a way of not only identifying but universalizing my symptoms: I was afloat, adrift in an anxious world. How could I not be suffering from "free-floating anxiety"? And did I even perhaps feel a hint of pride in the name, and in its cause? As if to suffer from "free-floating anxiety," to be depressed in such a world as ours, was to proudly wear the self-identifying sign of sensitivity and election: the blue badge of art. I was a novelist, an artist—that was why I was depressed.

Except, maybe not. Because my book hadn't exactly been a success, had it? I had made sure of that, by running away from success. But was it only because I'd run away that the book hadn't been a success? Maybe it was also because it really wasn't a very good book. Maybe, in fact, it sucked. And maybe I sucked, too. Maybe that was why I was depressed. Not because I was afraid of success, but because my book and I sucked. I just wasn't a very good writer. Maybe it was as simple as that. After all, bad writers—those, at least, who were not self-deluded, who were sensitive, and intelligent, and honest with themselves—bad writers in touch with reality had sooner or later to come to grips with the fact that they were bad. Maybe that was what was happening with me. That would be enough to plunge anyone into a depression, wouldn't it? Though maybe—probably—it wasn't as simplistic and brutal as that. It wasn't really that I was a *bad* writer. It was just that I wasn't as good as I wanted to be. Not as good as I needed to be. Just not good enough.

In October 1980 I began reading scripts and novels for my father's agents. I was paid by the piece—$35 for a script, $40 for a novel (even though novels were several times longer than scripts)—and it was my job to synopsize the story and say whether or not it would make a good movie. It wasn't easy to condense a whole novel or would-be movie into a synopsis a few pages long. And what made it even harder was that it was very difficult for me, in my present state of mind, to concentrate on what I was reading. I found myself having to reread sentences and whole pages, taking extensive notes on stupid plot details I thought might be important but didn't trust myself to remember. I knew I was expending altogether too much effort on the slush-pile material I was given. But from another point of view, that was OK. It gave me something to do with my days. Driving into Beverly Hills to drop off my reader's reports and pick up more material made me feel like I had a job to do. It gave me a purpose, however trivial and limited. It was better than facing the gnawing stomach of dread every morning, with nothing before me but the prospect of same. And it was certainly better than trying to write while feeling that way—which I had been doing, fruitlessly. Now I gave up even attempting to write anything but synopses—which, depressing as it was, was actually an improvement over trying and failing to write something "creative." It's hard to be creative when you're struggling just to get through the day (unless you're a Dostoyevski). And Senator, I was no Dostoyevski. I was beginning, from within the isolated bubble of my former illusions, to come to grips with this.

That fall I took to running barefoot on the beach, then plunging into the ocean, which in October had begun to turn chilly. This masochistic exercise suited my state of mind very well—a form of hydrotherapy, I suppose. The dread of the plunge, the shock of the cold, the pride of small triumph when I emerged numbed and tingling from the water. I felt strong, for a change. The tide was beginning to turn. I was coming alive again, in fits and starts, cautiously—for I had grown accustomed to my depression, and was a little ambivalent about giving it up.

Looking back on those unhappy days now, from the vantage point of much unhappier ones—from the profound, irremediable sadness of having lost the woman whose love rescued me from that earlier unhappiness—I can't help feeling an odd comfort in the memory of that depressed time. After all, it was the time just before I met Diane. Love and happiness were right around the corner. I didn't know it then, but I know it now, and so that time has the special anticipatory quality of a prelude seen in retrospect: the time leading up to meeting Diane. Those overcast fall mornings and evenings, those hazy days of October sun, hold forever now the promise of being about to give Diane to me, to usher in the happiest period of my life—my "Major Period."

To look at it this way is not really to inject a false knowledge into my consciousness at the time. I know that I was not anticipating any great happiness back then. Though I felt I was growing stronger, less depressed, the gnawing was still there in the mornings, and things sometimes had a strange and spooky film of dread over them. I still felt shaky, bruised, and tender—an escapee from New York: from an unhappy relationship with a beautiful woman with whom I was incompatible; from the wear and tear of the city, especially the streets and subways—whose excitement I had drunk up only four years ago, but which now grated on my exposed nerve-endings. I was escaping, most of all, from the publication of my novel. I had dared someone to call my bluff, they had done so, and I had run crying home, back to Mommy and Daddy. That in itself was enough to make anyone depressed, even without the biochemical component.

Yet the sadness of that time is not only put in its place—its much smaller place—by the sadness of this time in which I write, this iron, empty, post-Diane time. It is also now impossible to remember that earlier time without seeing it as a prelude—perhaps even a necessary prelude—to the "time of Diane": to that happy, happy pocket of time when we first met, and fell in love, and began—naturally, almost unconsciously—to make a life together. A life that lasted 23½ years.

We met at an English pub in Santa Monica, The King's Head, in January of '81. It was the first (and last) time I ever picked anybody up. My friend Ned and I were wearing flashing red buttons on our jackets, and smoking Indonesian clove cigarettes (which I later learned were much more carcinogenic than regular cigarettes). Not too obvious. I noticed an attractive, petite woman with bobbed brown hair sitting with friends at a table nearby. She was looking around the room and sniffing. I raised my cigarette to identify myself. Did she smile at me? She must have, otherwise I never would have had the courage (even with the John Courage ale I was drinking) to go up to her. But I did. She was wearing a navy blazer over a white blouse. She had blue eyes. Despite the smile, she was reserved. (She was always reserved with people she didn't know well.) As it happened, she was a story editor at an independent production company. I was a freelance reader. Story editors employ readers. She said she didn't need any readers at the moment, but if she did, she would give me a call, and we exchanged numbers. The next day I called and asked for a date. My depression, it seems, had lifted.

The first time we slept together, the night of our second date, I noticed the scars on her wrists. All I said was, "Are you better now?" She nodded, with that direct, honest and vulnerable look I saw then for the first time. And I thought to myself, "This is the one for me."

If there was some irony in the recognition, it was outweighed by the simple, honest truth of intuition. For my wounds, such as they were, were still fresh. Hers—much deeper—were healed over now. But she knew. She knew about things much worse than anything I had ever experienced. I recognized that right away, and in the months and years that followed, I came to know the full story.

The scars on her wrists weren't from a serious suicide attempt, but only superficial slashes: a gesture of adolescent self-loathing (she was 16 at the time), a cry for help. They landed her in Mt. Sinai Psychiatric Unit in upper Manhattan, and then in Chestnut Lodge, the posh institute in Rockville, Maryland that had been the setting for *I Never Promised You a Rose Garden*. At Chestnut Lodge, in the late 60s, they didn't medicate their patients—not even the actively psychotic ones, which Diane was. (This practice has since changed.) Instead, they treated her symptoms—voices, paranoid delusions, vegetative depressions—mostly with psychotherapy. The talking cure, for someone who was drowning. Chestnut Lodge was considered one of the best psychiatric institutions in the country at the time. But it was the time of R.D. Laing, and schizophrenia—her diagnosis—was understood, by the more enlightened practitioners of the art, as a psychological and socio-logical illness. So she spent almost three years at Chestnut Lodge in a misery of untreated psychosis. During that time she managed, somehow, to attend classes at Georgetown University in litera-ture and art history, and even got As. She also worked on theat-rical productions and musical events at the hospital, did the art for the *Chestnut Lodge Newsletter* (I have a pile of them beside me as I write), and made love, outdoors, on a blanket in the woods, with someone I'll call Frank. He was the editor-in-chief of the newsletter, a Yale dropout and speed-freak from New Canaan, CT—whose mother responded, after he'd brought Diane home one weekend and asked what she thought of her, "Frank, you know how I feel about the Jewish people." It was an intense relationship, and they did a lot of crying. "More crying than fucking," Diane said. Frank got out of Chestnut Lodge before her, went into guerrilla theater, and brought home a mahogany-colored girlfriend from South India for his mother to meet.

Diane eventually prevailed on her parents, who by then had divorced, to take her out of Chestnut Lodge, where she wasn't getting any better. She went to live with her mother in New York City. By then it was 1969, and the maverick psychopharmacologist Nathan Kline was just beginning to introduce a new generation of neuroleptic medications. Diane became his patient, and began to feel better for the first time in years. It was then, during that period of reemergent lucidity, when she looked back on the years she'd missed in the hospital, and at the long road ahead, that she tried—seriously, this time—to kill herself. She swallowed a bottle of Seconal, washed it down with a half-bottle of Southern Comfort, put an old record on the phonograph, and lay down on the sofa. An alert neighbor heard the scratched record repeating over and over, and when Diane didn't answer the bell, or the knocks on the door, the neighbor called the police, who broke down the door and rushed her to the hospital—just in time.

After that, there was no looking back. It was all a gift, and she made the most of it. But I can't help thinking that this second gift, so fortuitously bestowed on her after she'd done her best to return the first one, was only a mid-term loan, subject to recall at any time. Which is just how it happened. She was diagnosed with breast cancer at age 50, and died at 54. Even before she was diagnosed, she would sometimes mention a palm reader she'd gone to as a young woman, who'd told her she wouldn't live long.

Because of what she'd been through, she sympathized with my own bout of depression—mild compared to her odyssey, but she never said that. She just let me know that she understood. She understood so much. At last! Someone who really understood, intuitively, implicitly. I had never had that feeling before. And she had the same feeling. "It was like coming home," she said. That put it exactly right. I had supposedly come home from New York the previous summer—ostensibly in triumph, really in flight; but home turned out to be a very unhappy place, because I was bringing myself along, and I was not, at that time of my life, someone you would want to bring home with you. So coming home was not what it should have been—until I met Diane, and she became home. I signed my first Valentine's Day card to her "Your Permanent Date." "How did you know?" she would say. But it was a rhetorical question, because we both knew, without even thinking about it.

The April after we met, I got an ugly studio apartment on Hollywood Blvd., just west of La Brea (paying the rent with the reader's job I'd recently started at Warner Brothers), but I spent nearly every night at Diane's apartment in West Hollywood. The following Thanksgiving I moved in with her. I remember the time in that apartment as one of the happiest of my life. What a change from the summer and fall of 1980! Love had come and surprised us both. "I wasn't even looking for anyone," she used to say, when we'd remember those early days together. "I'd been out with so many creeps I really wasn't interested anymore."

"So why'd you go out with me?"

"Because you kept me laughing." That was my ace in the hole—the Pagliacci Effect.

I remember being struck, in those first weeks and months of knowing her, by her confiding of trivial things, the mundane, personal details of her everyday life: the errands she'd run, the phone calls she had to make—all of those little things that, if I had not been in love with her, would have struck me as boring. (And which actually did strike me as boring. But they had a charm and interest nonetheless, because they were part of her, who was not boring at all, and whose sudden and unexpected appearance in my life was a cause of frequent wonder to me.) They were details that I would have kept to myself, thinking they were not worth mentioning. But she thought otherwise. This, finally, was intimacy: the sharing not just of our bodies, but of all the little trivialities of a life in common. She was not afraid of emotional intimacy, unlike my previous girlfriend—and unlike me, too. My condescending superiority to the mention of trivial details was perhaps an expression of that fear.

I used to tell her, as I slowly learned to accept our intimacy and not be embarrassed by it (though I was always a little embarrassed by it, which is why I would often squint and grimace when we embraced standing up; "I can feel you grimacing," she would say)—I used to tell her there were two persons who had taught me how to love: she and Mae, our tricolor Welsh corgi (who once happened to lick my toes while I was masturbating. It was an accident, but I did not stop her.).

Diane didn't go that far. She didn't have to. Her lack of sexual inhibition wasn't based on kinkiness, or a studied adventurousness. In bed she was as direct and straightforward as she was outside of it. The difference was that the emotional reserve she kept for her dealings with the outside world was dispensed with in bed. Whereas I was the opposite: unguarded in public, but tending to be embarrassed, prudish, or mechanical during sex. I was known on occasion to burst into hysterical childish giggles when she would reach over and gently, with one of her direct and slightly humorous looks, put her hand on my penis.

"Oh God," she would say, amid my uncontrollable laughter, "here we go again. You're such a baby. Why are you such a baby?"

Exercise and red wine helped the process of disinhibition. She liked it when I went running, or biking, or swimming. She liked the clingy black biking shorts I wore, though she lamented the fact that when she went to cup my ass inside them, there was no ass to cup. "God, you really do have no ass," she would say, as if this were a continual revelation to her, and she might have made a mistake in choosing such a partner. (I, on the other hand, was grateful to have no such problem with her: She had a lovely ass.) And when I came back from swimming in the chlorinated pool she would nuzzle me around the ears and whisper, "Mmmm, your ears smell like come."

She did not drink (her psychiatric medication precluded alcohol, and she didn't enjoy the feeling anyway), but she liked it when I drank a little. Especially red wine, which we both thought had an aphrodisiac effect. When we went out to an Italian restaurant and I had red wine she would say, "Drink up," with a glint in her eyes. And not long after, at home, in bed, both of us in a frenzy, she would sometimes gasp, "I want you to come on my breasts! Come all over my breasts!" And sometimes I would. But not usually. Because I liked to come inside her, and hear her moaning, and then muffle her moans with my mouth, so our Armenian neighbors downstairs (who were also our landlords; by then we were living in East Hollywood) wouldn't hear. But in the early, pre-Armenian days, when we were living on Sweetzer, in West Hollywood, in the first year of our love, I wasn't nearly so careful. I would let 'er rip, and her friend Ellie, who lived in the apartment across the way, would sometimes hear her at night, and told her so. Diane was embarrassed, and after that she made a deliberate (but not always successful) effort to be quieter when we made love. My male pride was a little disappointed. But I didn't need to hear her moaning to know she was coming. In her censored, unvoiced, "muffled mode" she would rasp breathily, in a long, drawn-out exhalation of release, or gasp in short, sharp, staccato bursts. Then I knew I'd hit the spot. (Maybe Ellie did, too. The thought of it turned me on even more.)

The sex was always good between us, even though the frequency may not have been as much as she wanted, because of my compulsive masturbation—no longer idly, to the prosody of Horace or Homer, as in Exeter days, but now concentratedly, in the bathroom, miserable wretch that I was, while she slept (or while I thought she slept), to various collections of erotica, edited by the multi-talented therapist and author Lonnie Barback, Ph.D. Pathetic. And what a waste. It shamed and guilted me at the time. But now I just feel a deep regret—all that time selfishly spent pleasuring myself, when I could have been pleasuring both of us. But although she would occasionally mention something: "I felt the bed shaking;" "Did you do it in the bathroom last night?"—it was always with a smile, and never in a way to add to my guilt and shame. Quite the opposite. She didn't want me to feel bad, so she would say something reassuring like, "It's normal," or "Everybody does it." (She had a vibrator that she occasionally used when I was out of the house. It now sits gathering dust on a bookshelf in our bedroom. My bedroom, I mean. Why haven't I thrown it out? For the same reason I still haven't thrown out, or donated, many of her clothes and shoes: Because these things once touched her.)

I knew she was hurt, and could not help, despite all her under-standing, taking my masturbation personally. One time she said, "I guess I'm just not enough for you."

"It's not that," I said. "It's that being with you gets me all revved up."

"So why don't you wake me up, then?"

"I don't know," I lied. But I did know. It was because, sometimes—all too often—I would rather masturbate. I even sometimes waited for her to go to sleep so I could do it. (The psychiatric medication she was on made her tire early, and sleep heavily.) What a waste—and what a failure. And now Diane isn't here to tell me different.

But despite my failure to stop masturbating, and denying my love to the woman I loved, the sexual bond between us was strong—at least up until the mastectomy and chemotherapy; and then again, though in a different way, for the three years of remission, until the cancer came back, a year before she died. But from the very beginning, it was always more than sex. It was love.

Not love at first sight, exactly, but something deeper, more unexpected, more mysterious. A recognition of sorts, the recognition of "coming home." And this recognition kept getting stronger over the years, through career changes, and graduate school, and parenthood, and the academic job market, and a move across country, and my writing. Always, my writing. My unsuccessful yet persistent (compulsive? masturbatory?) writing.

Although my meeting Diane coincided with another recognition as well—the recognition that I was a failure as a writer—it was also she who, more than anything else, made me feel like a writer. Bellow said, "All a writer needs is a woman to tell him he's a writer." Diane was that woman for me. Of course, I didn't believe her—but that wasn't her fault. It felt good to hear her say it anyway, and to know that she believed it. I knew she was no fool, and that if she believed it, maybe someday, after that early false start, it might even come true.

9

Failure in Hollywood

"All gratulant if rightly understood."
William Wordsworth, *The Prelude*, Book 13 (1805)

I mentioned there was no follow-up to the publication of my first novel—no second novel ready, or even half-ready, for publication. Not then, or in the 25 years (and counting) that followed. Yet in another sense—an even more pathetic one, perhaps—there was a follow-up. Largely on the strength of having published a novel with a major publisher—that, and the fact that my father was a fairly well-known screenwriter—I got a job as a reader (the official name was "Story Analyst") at Warner Brothers, in the Story Department of their Features Division. My having published a novel thus qualified me to read, synopsize, and comment on other people's writing—specifically, on screenplays, novels, nonfiction, and plays submitted to the studio executives and the Story Editor (head of the Story Department) for movie consideration. I went from being a writer to a synopsizer of other people's writing. I made bad scripts sound better than they were, and good scripts sound worse.

Yet I have largely fond memories of my five and a half years at Warner Brothers. The main reason they are fond is because they constitute the first part of my "Major Period," the first part of my life with Diane. Memories from the "Major Period" are now overwhelmingly fond ones—even the memories of her illness, suffering, and death—because they are still, after all, memories of her, and all memories of her are precious. The memories from the "Major Period," even the bad ones, have come to take on, and be suffused by, the predominant "Diane atmosphere" that interpenetrates and informs all those years; and the retrospective power of the "Diane atmosphere" to place individual painful memories within a larger context of happiness is a comforting and sustaining one.

The Warner Brothers job had its satisfactions and its miseries. I won't attempt to separate them completely, since they often went together in the way that I experienced them. The small satisfactions I experienced in that job were felt to be those of a failure, a failed writer. They were thus tempered by a larger dissatisfaction, while the larger dissatisfaction was mitigated by the smaller ones. Of course, there were days when the miseries overshadowed the satisfactions, and vice versa. But on the whole, despite my general dissatisfaction with myself, I was still more satisfied with the job than I had any right to be, as a writer; and the knowledge of that satisfaction itself contributed to my larger dissatisfaction.

"As a writer"? Perhaps I should have said "former writer." I was a traitor, of sorts, now working for "management" (the studio execs and Story Editor who employed me). Though technically speaking I was still "labor," a member of a labor union, Story Analysts Local 854, part of I.A.T.S.E. Because it was a union job, the pay and benefits were quite good. This was one of the sources of my satisfaction, since I'd never had a job with benefits before, or that paid so well. True, as the job went on I began to take the pay and benefits more for granted. But I have never been one to take things entirely for granted. My sense of my situation in life has always—even in childhood—been of the "Sword of Damocles" or "It Could Be Worse" variety. This probably is connected to an appetite for guilt and suffering, which enables me to easily imagine a turnaround in my fortunes (a turnaround such as has now occurred, in the worst possible way, with Diane's death). For whatever reasons, I never quite got used to the comforts of having a regular (weekly!) paycheck and generous medical benefits—including psychotherapy benefits, of which (it will come as no surprise) I readily availed myself.

My office at Warner Brothers was across the alleyway from Clint Eastwood's Malpaso Productions office, and I soon saw the need to develop a "Clint Eastwood smile" for the times, once every few months, when I happened to see him. By "Clint Eastwood smile" I do not mean a smile in imitation of his; I mean a smile in response to his presence. The smile was casual, yet exquisitely alert. It signaled to Clint (at least I hoped it did) the following state of affairs concerning myself: "Of course I recognize you. How could I not? But I am too cool to make a big deal out of it. Yet I am not so much of a fool, either, as not to register the excitement of seeing you on a regular basis on the lot, where we both work." Had I seen any of Clint Eastwood's movies? Of course not. I was too much of an intellectual snob. Also, I was not really a movie buff. In fact, I was probably the least knowledgeable about movies of all the ten or so readers on staff. What I liked was simply the *idea* of Clint Eastwood, which I had garnered from others: his unpretentiousness; his self-deprecating humor; his conventional masculine strengths, best admired by someone like me at a distance; his professionalism as a director; his unassuming mediocrity as an actor. (Am I too tolerant, even fond, of unassuming mediocrity? Is there hypocrisy in this stance?) Whatever the case, it didn't prevent me from getting pleasure in seeing Clint Eastwood around the lot, or in working the smile for him. I don't believe he ever returned, or even noticed, my smile. (Come to think of it, I don't believe he ever noticed me.) But that was irrelevant, and its irrelevance only underlined the importance of the smile for me. The "Clint Eastwood smile" became an existential statement—though a light-hearted one, shared and appreciated by Diane—about the unlikely absurdity of my presence in the vicinity of Clint Eastwood.

My office, across the alleyway from Clint's—we were on a first-name basis only, as he would say, "in my mind"—was "a modest affair, but mine" (Herr Settembrini, in *The Magic Mountain*. The juxtaposition of Thomas Mann and Clint Eastwood pleases me.). All of the "on-lot" readers' rooms were in a building that had formerly housed the Makeup Department. Each had a bathroom, even a shower. My office had a tall-backed, reclining swivel chair with a ripped vinyl seat, a black-and-white fabric upholstered sofa, a weathered old wooden writing desk with an oversized, ugly ceramic desk lamp on top of it, and a beat-up but indestructible "C Model" IBM electric typewriter (pre-Selectric). Other readers asked for, and received, newer furnishings. I never did. Why? Because I didn't want them. I suppose I also thought it possible that my request, unlike the other readers' requests, would be denied. But I don't think I really believed that. I knew it would take some haggling, though, and I didn't want to haggle. Those with Swords of Damocles above their heads are not disposed to haggle. (They call it "haggling." Others, of a brighter disposition, would call it "asking for what they are entitled to." But for losers, there is no entitlement. Losers have no rights. They have only the handout, which they are greatly appreciative of—as I was greatly appreciative of my job, and my office, and the occasional opportunity afforded me to exercise my "Clint Eastwood smile.")

The view from my office, like the furniture, wasn't much: a few stucco, tile-roofed buildings across the alleyway, and the usually sunny-smoggy sky. The smog in Burbank was worse than the smog over the hill in East Hollywood, where Diane and I lived while I worked at Warner Brothers (and for many years thereafter). I remember the sound of the crows in the pine trees, and those long, hot summer afternoons, when I was prone to napping under the large desk, after the tedium of reading and synopsizing became unbearable. The long stretch between lunch and 5 p.m. was especially rough if I was reading science fiction, always the hardest material to synopsize. I gritted my teeth and plowed through it; when that was no longer possible, I napped. (No one saw me napping, since I was under the desk.)

Although every day was largely the same in terms of routine—read the script, write it up, deliver it to the Story Department office and make copies, go to lunch, once or twice a week go for a swim at the Y in Glendale (next to Burbank) on my lunch hour—every day was also slightly different, because of what I was working on (or "covering," in readers' parlance). Every script or novel was its own world, which I would enter into for the duration of the coverage. Sometimes these worlds were of an oppressive badness (especially the scripts)—badly conceived, badly written—but they were still worlds: someone's vision of a movie, a story that might, just might, cause a movie to be made that audiences would become part of for a couple of hours. And I was the guinea pig for these possible movies, these possible shared worlds. I could not help entering into them, for better or worse. I was a conscientious, slow reader. I read every page, even every word, of what I was covering, no matter how bad it was, and I made sure that my synopses made sense—even when the story I was covering didn't. I inhabited each world I was covering, however impoverished it might be.

But not entirely. That was where the real interest lay. Part of my reading consciousness always remained detached from the story I was covering, attentive instead to the "scene of reading:" the sky above Burbank, the tile roofs of the buildings across the alleyway, the crows in the pine trees, and also the imaginings and fantasies I would have while I was reading. These usually had nothing to do with the content of the material. This "internal scene of reading," I will call it, has long been a peculiarity of mine. I tend to associate the reading of particular books, usually obligatory school texts but sometimes pleasure reading as well, with particular locations from childhood. The locations generally have nothing whatsoever to do with the content of the books; often they are remembered parts of streets and freeways, or friends' houses and yards. For instance, when I was reading Caesar's *Gallic Wars* at Exeter, my "internal scene of reading" was the wide bend of Sunset Boulevard in Brentwood, where it curves around Paul Revere Junior High. Xenophon's *Anabasis* was the Sunset overpass at the San Diego Freeway. *The Magic Mountain* was (and still is, no matter how many times I re-read it to teach it) Tracy Hudson's living room, and the view out the sliding-glass door to the pool. Horace's *Odes* was the street outside Jim Schram's, off Amalfi in the upper Palisades. (Right near where Thomas Mann lived!) Such locations would provide the "inner scene" of what I was reading. This is not to say that I did not visualize the actual setting and events of the story. I did. But always, as a backdrop to the actual settings, would be the internal, autobiographical settings, which were more important to me.

The process of attaching "internal scenes" to my reading was automatic. Some people I've told about it have thought that it serves a mnemonic function, which seems plausible. But the possible explanation for the "internal scenes" is not as interesting to me as the way they filled those long summer afternoons in Burbank, so that my covering of every script became associated with a procession of banal yet comforting images from my early years. The memory of that office in Burbank has now become another such image, suffused by the "Diane-atmosphere" of which I was almost entirely unconscious at the time, and which seems as precious now as it was taken for granted then. Because although I might not have taken my job for granted, I did take our life together for granted. Perhaps because I felt secure in it (they say that people in good marriages tend to take each other for granted), whereas I did not feel secure in my job.

This was because I knew that my taste in movies was eccentric, uncommercial, literary—the kiss of death, if I had been a studio executive or story editor (which of course I never could have been, with tastes like mine). I had been called on the carpet a couple of times by the first Story Editor I worked under at Warner Brothers. She didn't like my occasional big words and intellectual style. "You're not reading for New York intellectuals, Josh," she admonished me. (In my perverse way, I took this as a compliment.) Despite my intellectuality, though, I was not overly critical of what I read, but rather, over-enthusiastic about the occasional worthy script that, for one reason or another, didn't stand a chance of being produced by anyone at Warner Brothers. This was also a problem. To be a successful reader, you had not only to be able to read the scripts themselves, but also the executives' probable response to those scripts (as well as their probable response to your response!). You had to know something about the executives' own tastes, and the movies they had helped to produce, both at Warner Brothers and elsewhere.

The Story Editor knew all this, of course, but it hadn't occurred to me to ask her—nor would I have wanted to, even if it had. For obvious reasons, I was ill at ease with her, and with the executives as well, on the few occasions when I had cause to come into contact with them—a combination of inferiority, superiority, and just general neurosis at that time in my life (late 20s, early 30s) about my place in the world, let alone on the Warner Brothers lot. I have never known how to play politics, or wanted to learn. Of course, if you want something badly enough, you learn how to play enough politics to get it. I didn't. I had never intended to work in Hollywood, and had more or less fallen into the job. I could appreciate that it was a nice job to have fallen into, and I didn't want to lose it. But I didn't want to advance through the ranks, either—to Story Editor, then executive, as some readers did; nor did I want to be a screenwriter, as others did.

So my work at Warner Brothers always lacked that larger purpose—an ambition in the movie business—that drove my colleagues through those long afternoons, and made them more interested in studio projects and politics. It is surprising I lasted as long as I did without getting fired; though, since it was a

union job, it wasn't easy to fire people. You had to show they
were incompetent, and I certainly wasn't that. If anything, I was
overly conscientious, as if to make up for my eccentricities of
taste.

But it was the wrong job for me, and I grew an ulcer to prove
it. I had gotten myself into a perilous form of second-guessing,
whereby if I liked something, that must mean it was uncommercial, and I couldn't recommend it; whereas if I didn't like
something because it was too crassly commercial, I thought I
was obligated, by the money-making principles of the business,
to recommend it. I began to doubt my instincts and my taste, and
that is never a good thing for a stomach.

The situation improved when the bitchy Story Editor left
and was replaced by one of the readers, the one most adept at
playing the political game, but who was also an easygoing, nice
guy—not the sort to call anyone on the carpet (or if he did, at
least to do it nicely). When he left for an executive position at
Universal, he was replaced by his assistant, who continued the
benign administration of the Story Department. By this time
(mid-80s), Warner Brothers had developed the reputation of
being the best story department in Hollywood to work in. My
stomach agreed—no more need for crazy second-guessing—but
my conscience was still uneasy, not so much about what I was
doing as what I wasn't doing. I wasn't developing my mind.
I wasn't working towards a worthwhile goal—or towards any
goal, really. It wasn't enough to be the philosopher of the Warner
Brothers Story Department.

I had been taking extension classes in philosophy at U.C.L.A.
for several years, ever since reading Jacob Needleman's *The
Heart of Philosophy*, which I'd seen one day in the window of a
Crown Books on Western Avenue, while walking to get a haircut.
I started reading it during the haircut, and couldn't stop. (The
barber, Mits Akino, was later murdered during an armed robbery
of his shop. I went to get a haircut and found the shop locked,
and a sign posted on the window, which I read with horrified

disbelief: "Anyone having information in the murder of Mits Akino, please contact the L.A.P.D....")

The excitement generated by *The Heart of Philosophy* led to other books by Needleman, then extension classes in existentialism, ethics, and other topics in philosophy. Sometimes, on my (extended) lunch hour, I would take long walks to a used bookstore on Magnolia Blvd. to browse the shelves, letting the reverie prompted by the titles of serious, scholarly books and soul-nourishing novels replace the profane images of the coverage I was doing back in the office. These walks to and from the bookstore were important to me. Not only did they give me a break from the drudgery of doing coverage; they also allowed me to "contemplate about things," as I used to say as a child, when I felt the need to go off somewhere and just let my mind drift, think things over, fall into a reverie. Often the place I went was the bathroom, where I took an inordinate amount of time, holding back my bowel movement as I "contemplated about" various things in my life. The pleasure derived by such eccentric behavior was both physical and imaginative.

This "contemplating about things" continued now in my lunchtime walks in Burbank (though without the bowel element), and provided the imaginative wherewithal to get through the rest of the afternoon. To project, in my imagination, from my burrow of an office, beyond that afternoon, and similar future afternoons, towards an imagined future when Diane and I would embark from southern California, on a different sort of life altogether. A life back East, I hoped, though I had absolutely no idea, as yet, how I could make that happen. A life where there were real seasons, and cold, true cold, with snow and ice on the ground, instead of this oppressive sunshine "too smiling for our reason," as Hardy wrote. Now, living on Long Island, I love the sunshine, but back then I could not appreciate it, not only because it was taken for granted, but also because it was part of a place, a life, that I had become bored and dissatisfied with. Thus the seeds of an imagined future life—a life that ten years later became a reality—were planted back in those days of reverie, walking the banal streets of Burbank and wishfully browsing in that little used bookstore on Magnolia Blvd.

The combination of the sense of hope and failure that I felt on those walks was an interesting thing. The two senses played off one another in ways that were fruitful (or seedful). I took walks to allay the boredom, letting my mind wander, reverize, and "contemplate about things" in ways that are not possible when one is sitting—especially when one is sitting in one's office doing coverage. As Rousseau and Wordsworth knew (though at the time I didn't know that they knew it, since this was before grad school and my discovery of Romanticism), the mind often works best when the body also is in motion. I felt the urgent need to be in motion somewhere, since in other ways I felt stuck, going nowhere, unproductive, eking out my days under the smoggy skies of Burbank. My promise as a writer was frittering itself away, more and more every day.

So where did I find hope in those days? Oddly enough, I found a sort of hope in the everyday things I encountered on my walks: in the Burbank storefronts, where I imagined the lives of the people who worked in the businesses there; and in the modest, nondescript houses with their neat, manicured yards. Who lived in those houses? Their lives surely must be cramped, limited, imaginatively impoverished: conservative, Republican, boring. Yet what did I know? I was just a passerby, a tourist of sorts—a tourist in Burbank! (And not even the Hollywood part, but the residential part.)

Yet the tourist perspective was not to be discounted. The tourist perspective gave novelty, interest, and life to the familiar and everyday. It may be that the lives of the Burbank denizens, the lives lived in those nondescript houses, behind those storefronts, held their own dramas, hopes, dreams, disappointments—their own great expectations for the future, their own excitements of the day. Indeed, it had to be. How could it be otherwise? It was this perception—the realization of my own false assumptions, my own impoverishment of the imagination, my constitutional inability to think small rather than large—it was this thought that gave me a kind of hope on those walks. Not the hope of great expectations, of great achievements someday, of an escape from the present life into a different sort of life altogether—more dramatic, more arduous, more vital. But the hope, rather, of immanence: the smaller hope of accepting one's life in the present for what it was, with its small pleasures felt, its responsibilities discharged, its difficulties dealt with and overcome, or simply endured. The hope given by endurance, rather than by triumph or escape.

These imaginings were fueled by my philosophical readings, of course; but they were also influenced by my other reading, my reading on the job. My work as a reader had its own small pleasures: the pleasures of work well executed (often better than the material deserved), the coverage conscientiously and professionally done. Although the reading of scripts and books that did not interest me often seemed pointless and dispiriting, an exercise in futility, the writing up of this reading was almost always satisfying, to some degree. Perhaps this had to do with the bringing of order to chaos; or with the dutiful (though inevitably distorting) reflection of quality in a lesser medium (the reader's report); or, in the comment section of the coverage, and the satisfactions therein of bestowing praise and thoughtful criticism. But I think the feeling of satisfaction was more basic than that. It had to do with the fact that in a business where, at the studio end at least, there was so much abstraction, so many empty and thoughtless words, so much talking on the phone and in meetings—so much bullshit, in short—at the end of the day, or at some point during the day, I could point to the reader's report I had produced. That was not bullshit; or if it was, because the script that I was covering was bullshit, then at least it was a kind of bullshit that was less misleading and more concrete than a phone conversation or a meeting. The words in my report were not words of air; I had gotten it down on paper. Which is what, after all, a writer does—even if it is somebody else's words he is getting down.

Which brings me to another aspect of my failure at this time: it was humbling. Perhaps it was this humbling aspect that caused me to think twice about the modest, banal houses of Burbank, to see them in a different light. My job as a reader was a humbling one. Many of the scripts I had to synopsize were awful—what one of my professors at Berkeley (Thomas Flanagan, who taught the Proust course, and went on to become a distinguished historical novelist) would have called "a besmirching experience." The proud writer in me resented having to do such work—resented it, was ashamed of it, saw in it an indication of how far I had fallen, and in how short a time. In August of '80 I was a just-published first novelist; by February of '81, I was a Story Analyst. (The euphemism of this title, intended to lend more dignity to the job, had the opposite effect, like all euphemisms, and only brought attention to its paltriness.) I could still call myself a published novelist, but I didn't feel like one. I felt like a failed novelist. Yet there was something in that feeling "that did not displease me," as La Rochefoucauld would say. I was being punished for my former arrogance, and in an appropriate way. The philosopher in me could look at this with a wry eye and appreciate that it was as it should be—or at least as it should be for me, who was not only something of a masochist but also a believer in poetic justice.

So why did I not try to write a screenplay, like so many other readers? Wouldn't that have been better than synopsizing other people's scripts? It was worthier work, surely—creative, rather than regurgitory—and it paid much better. For someone who could write, and was already working in a studio (not to mention across the alley from Clint Eastwood), writing a script would seem to be a no-brainer. And that was the first strike against it: other people were doing it. The elitist in me has always shied away from popular pursuits, opinions, tastes. I am no longer proud of this trait. It has closed me off from the enjoyment of many things—books, movies, music, teenage sex—just because they were popular, and the things that people "were doing." Though maybe it is really more perversity than elitisim: an unaccountable perversity that steers me away from what is commonly enjoyed.

What is critically (and especially intellectually) acclaimed is another thing altogether. Here I am a strict, credulous conformist. It is enough for me to spot, with a twinge of eggheaded excitement, the words "major achievement," "magisterial study," "definitive work" on the back cover of a book for me to plunk down my money, no questions asked. Then I give myself over to a higher intellectual power—especially if it contains citations of reviews by Louis Menand, from the *New York Review of Books*, the *American Scholar*, the *Times Literary Supplement*, or anything with the following words: "philosophy," "history," "journal," "quarterly," and/or "review." I am putty in their hands. (My ideal publication would probably be something like the *Quarterly Journal and Review of the Philosophy of History*. Would I actually read it? Of course not; but I would feel much better—more intelligent, validated, and secure—just being a subscriber. This feeling would be what the existentialists called "Bad Faith." But that would not be enough for me not to feel it.)

I end up not reading a substantial majority of the books that I buy (see Chapter 13). I know I would have a lot more fun if I just went with the popular stuff. By the same token, I would have a lot more fun if I weren't me. The thing is, "fun" isn't really fun for me; and what isn't fun, is (sort of). But as W.C. Fields said when he kicked Baby Leroy into the fireplace, "Who knows what's funny?" Fun is not the point. So what is the point? The Grand Triumverate (remember that?): suffering, guilt, and failure. Let's party!

The second strike against my writing a screenplay was that screenplays are mostly plot, and I wasn't very good at plot. Besides, what I wanted to write was mostly not plot at all. I wanted to be free to wander amid the "scenes of my writing," in

the same way as in my lunchtime walks in Burbank; to stroll and
meander in my imaginary (but not necessarily fictional) world,
and "contemplate about" things and people and places and ideas,
using writing as my sidewalk. The concentrated dramatic form
was not for me. And in any case, the last thing I wanted to do
in my time away from my scriptreading job was to be trying to
write scripts.

The last and biggest strike against me as a screenwriter was my
screenwriter father, whose dictum I had taken to heart: "If you
want to be a writer, be a *real* writer." He didn't need to add "not
a *screenwriter*." And the final coda, "like me," also went without
saying—a sort of Hollywood version of Brando's famous "I
coulda been a contender" speech. (Though my father liked to
see himself more as a Willy Loman than a Terry Molloy.)

Did he really believe what he said? I think so. Did he feel
he'd made a mistake himself by becoming a screenwriter instead
of a "real writer"? That is harder to answer. He'd published a
novel with Viking in 1946, *End Over End*, based on his experiences as a prisoner of war in Italy and Germany. He'd written it
in prison camp, on precious, hidden pieces of unruled foolscap,
in a minuscule hand, to save paper. (I keep the manuscript in
the room where I write.) It was one of the first American novels
about World War II, predating Mailer's *The Naked and the Dead*
by two years. (My dad had known Mailer at Harvard, where
they both wrote for the *Advocate*.) *End Over End* came out to
good reviews, and he'd gotten an advance from Viking to write
a nonfiction book on Palestine. My father had an ambivalent
attitude toward his own Jewishness, which went along with his
facetiously anti-Semitic attitude toward other Jews—especially
those less assimilated (and less self-hating) than he. He was
always careful to emphasize that his second book was to have
been on pre-1948 Palestine, not Israel. (He had visited Palestine
with his grandmother, in the 30s.)

But he never wrote that second book. Instead, he began
writing for radio, then came out to Hollywood to help create the

"Sgt. Preston of the Yukon" TV series. Not long after that, he began writing movies. He had a productive collaboration—and a close, long-standing friendship—with Robert Wise (they did five films together), and with Mark Robson (they did two, including one about the assassination of Gandhi, *Nine Hours to Rama*—that was why we went to India).

By most measurements, my father was a successful screen-writer. Yet he sometimes thought of himself as a failure, someone who'd failed to be a "real writer." Thus his famous dictum to me, as much a display of half-serious self-laceration (he was prone to that) as a piece of fatherly advice. Was my father, then, my primal "figure of failure"? The theatrical nature of his dictum suggested that he didn't entirely believe it himself. But it played well, and steered me, his son, in the direction of the (perhaps) more "substantial" achievement he'd envisioned for himself at Harvard, and during and after the war. That vision was expressed epigrammatically, in his copy of F.O. Matthiessen's *American Renaissance*. "Mattie," who'd been his tutor at Harvard, had inscribed it: "To Nelson, whose talents will be heard from."

"That's the saddest thing of all," my father said.

But if the true voice of failure is silent, then my father's ironic, ongoing commentary on his own fate as a writer would seem to preclude him from that category. One must invent another category for him—that of the self-perceived "figure of pathos." The semi-facetious, theatricalized portrayal of this figure could be seen not only in his reaction to the Matthiessen inscription, but also in such things as the notes he used to leave around the house on E. 64th Street, carefully concealed in strategic places, for my mother to find (though sometimes others, like my grand-mother or uncle, would find them instead): under the toilet seat, stuck to the bathroom mirror, inside her favorite egg cup. The notes read simply "Pity Poor Nelson," and were apparently inspired by *Death of a Salesman*, whose opening night they'd attended together, along with my grandmother and uncle (a truly failed lawyer, inventor, and investor, whose succinct evaluation, as they were walking stunned up the aisle after the performance, was: "That *stunk*. You can do better than *that*, Nels."). Or in "The Drop," a dance he did to the music of Charles Trenet, in which his trousers ended up rucked around his ankles. Or in various references to "the empty bunk" (belonging to the war buddy who never returned from the mission), "the spent arrow, the spoken word, the lost opportunity" (three things that never come back), and "riding on a smile and a shoeshine" (Willy Loman again).

The "figure of pathos" was to be distinguished from the "figure of failure" (for example, Paul) by the ironic self-consciousness that was fundamental to the former. The "figure of pathos" was a literary creation, in control of his fate; the "figure of failure" was neither. I understood the "figure of pathos" to be merely a theatrical representation, whereas the "figure of failure" was the real thing. Both had their effect on me; but my father, after all, was my father, and it was his example that I sought to emulate.

Yet despite the fact that I have followed his warnings about screenwriting, I have no doubt that he would be aghast at this book I am writing—starting with the title itself. I can hear him asking, in that impatient, critical tone he had, and with a grimace, his hand rubbing his furrowed brow, "Is it funny, at least? Did you make it funny?"

To which I reply, addressing him by the infantile term of endearment that neither of us ever outgrew, "I hope so, Gog. I tried."

I mentioned earlier that there was something about my failure as a novelist that, in the words of La Rochefoucauld, "did not displease me." Yet there was more to my failure to be displeased by my own failure than just masochism, or a perverse sense of poetic justice. There was also a sort of imaginative curiosity, the same kind of curiosity, perhaps, that animated my interest in the banal houses of Burbank. A curiosity directed not just at the thought of other lives, but at my own life, regarded as if it were the life of another: my life seen from the outside, by me. This peculiar curiosity may be related to a way I have of regarding other people whom I have an instinctively condescending first reaction to—the homeless, say, or the handicapped. The first instinctive reaction of pity, or horror, or both, is almost immediately replaced by a more conscious, rationalizing response: "Maybe it's not what you think. It is bad, it is horrible, yes—but maybe not exactly in the ways that you think. Maybe their experience, the reality of their day-to-day existence, has aspects and dimensions, both for better and worse, that you cannot imagine. Your knowledge of what their life is like is incomplete, just as an outside onlooker's knowledge of your life would be incomplete."

But what if that outside onlooker was me? What then? Might it not be possible for this sense of my life, as seen by the outside onlooker, to give me hope? The same kind of hope that I got when I regarded, from the "tourist perspective," the modest homes of Burbank, which I might otherwise—which in fact I did—find depressing?

This kind of outsider's curiosity, when directed at upsetting things you wouldn't normally want to think about, I call the "curiosity of the horrible", or "the curiosity of disaster." It sounds rather heartless, but it isn't. Detached, yes—but ultimately not, because it is not aimed at scientific understanding, but at finding a way to live one's life in the here and now that is both philo-sophical and hopeful. The knowledge that my life, my daily ups and downs (especially the downs), can be seen from the outside as well as experienced from the inside, gives me a perspective on them that is comforting.

It may be, though, that I have now taken my "curiosity of the horrible" too far. Diane died three years ago of metastatic breast cancer. She was diagnosed almost five years before she died, so I had time not only to imagine her death, but to be curious about how I would survive it. That is horrible: not just what I was curious about—the horribleness of her illness, and her death,

and what life without her would be like for me and our son, who
was not yet 17 when she died—but the fact of my curiosity itself
is horrible. Detached, heartless, cold. I never told her, of course.
My curiosity was a dirty little secret that I kept hidden, even
from myself; it was too dirty even to write about in my journal.
Though it was not a secret to my "outside regarder." Because it
was, after all, his curiosity, which he was not quite able to conceal
from my "inner experiencer."

I realize that all of this talk of "inner/outer" may be sheer
mystification—just a way of rationalizing what is monstrous
in me. And it is not my business to rationalize anything, only
to disclose it. And to reflect on it. So what does my reflection tell me? It tells me that I have a tendency to imagine the
horrible, the disastrous happening to me and those I love, as if
from the outside—as if it were happening to someone else: the
"outside regarder." As if it were not really me who was living
through Diane's cancer and death. No doubt this is a defensive
mechanism, a form of denial. Perhaps it is related to that
masochism, that wish for a cruel, impersonal reckoning ("poetic
justice") noted earlier. But again, I don't want to rationalize it.
It seems not to want justification, only confession. And like all
confessions, it comes out of a kind of hope—not so much the
hope of forgiveness, but of what forgiveness paves the way for:
hope for the future. My "curiosity of the horrible," my imagination of personal disaster, may come out of a need to imagine
what will happen if the worst comes to pass. If Diane should
die—what then? Well, I am now living in that "then." My daily
life consists of that "what."

After Diane had the second surgery, and they found that the
cancer had spread all over her abdomen ("like grains of millet,"
one of the surgeons said) and was inoperable, Zack, not yet 17,
stumblingly asked his uncle Robby, Diane's brother:

"You mean she might die?"

"She could," Robby replied.

He told me afterward that Zack received this information as

if it had never occurred to him before. That's what gets me more than anything: my son's innocence. His stumbling question. He apparently did not have the curiosity of the horrible, the imagination of disaster. Of course not. He was only 16.

With all of my horrible curiosity, one thing I have not been able to imagine is how I could have survived my own mother's death when I was 16. (She died shortly after I turned 41.) No amount of reverous walking in Burbank, or anywhere else, could ever help me imagine such a thing. I guess the outside regarder stops short when the object of observation is your own son.

There was another source of hope on those walks in Burbank, one that I wasn't fully conscious of at the time. This was the same source that flickered behind those tedious hours of reading in my office, and that flared up cheerfully every afternoon at the end of the workday, when it was time to go home: Diane. The taken-for-granted fact of our life together. It was she I left behind in the morning, and she I came back to in the evening. It was also she who called me in my office every day—sometimes several times a day—with this or that little instruction or bit of news. I remember I used to wonder why she called so much. Loneliness? Neediness? Boredom? Was this partly my fault? Despite the slight guilt that these questions brought, I also felt vaguely smug and superior because I didn't see, as she seemed to, the need to call at the slightest pretext. That must mean I was more self-sufficient, that I didn't need the regular contact with her over the course of the day that she needed with me. Sometimes I was annoyed by the calls, and was curt or dismissive, and then she was hurt.

The memory of this now doesn't make me feel particularly guilty or remorseful; those are feelings which—with one glaring exception, which I will tell in a later chapter—I don't associate with our life together. I mention her calls because they were part of a background, a horizon, that is now gone from my life. That background was Diane. It existed for me because she existed, because we had created a life together. Against this background everything else in my life took place, was imagined and planned and experienced and understood. But the background itself was taken for granted, and thus went unnoticed. My experience of it was unconscious, like the air I breathed, the body I was born with, the beating of my heart. In only a few years of being together we had become each other's living environment, so to speak, the taken-for-granted basis of a mutual existence. She, and our life together, were my "horizon of expectation:" the unnoticed but essential background against which all of my plans, imaginings, reveries, worries, and contemplations were projected. Despite my nagging feelings of failure in Burbank, despite my frustrations and dissatisfactions with the course (or careening) of my career, my wonderings and anxieties about the future, the "horizon of expectation" that was Diane, and us together, continued to exist as an ambient background glow covering all my days and nights. Before her, before our coming together, that glow had not existed. And now, after she has gone, it exists no more. The glow that I barely even noticed for 23 and a half years, but which was the foundation of my adult happiness, has now gone out of my life. But I know that it was there, as surely as I know that I breathe; and against the surety of that knowledge, against the memory of that glow, the sense of my failure, for once, seems beside the point.

10

My Failure as an Academic

A part from my failure to get into Harvard—which was perceived more as an existential failure, a failure of my being—my first failure as an academic was when I flunked my Ph.D. oral exam, in April of 1991. The shame of it is with me still. Exposed, finally, as the dummy, the fraud I had always known myself to be, and in front of the five professors I had chosen to be on my exam committee—the professors I held in highest regard, and who I wanted to hold me in high regard, too. They had now judged me as unfit to continue towards my doctoral degree. I would have to retake the qualifying exam, both the written and the oral sections, at a later date.

I walked around in a daze for a week, replaying over and over selected fragments of my debacle:

"Do you really believe that the 'Romantic self,' as you call it, is something that exists apart from language, from discursive practices?"

"Um...no, I guess not...."

"You say that Byron's narrative in *Don Juan* is 'dialogic,' in Bakhtin's sense of the word. But Bakhtin used this idea in reference to the novel, not poetry. So I'm wondering now what isn't 'dialogic,' according to your definition."

"Yes…I see your point…."

And then the clincher, from the 18th-century British literature scholar whom I held perhaps in highest esteem, because he seemed at once the most erudite and the most modest:

"Have you actually read all the books on your proposed reading list? Have you read, for example, *Ecce Homo*?"

"No."

"*The Antichrist*?"

"No."

"*Being and Time*?"

"Yes…I mean, well, the beginning…But I've read Steiner's book on Heidegger. Does that count?"

"*The Rebel*?"

"No."

"Anything by Gabriel Marcel?"

"No."

"Karl Jaspers?"

"No, not yet. But I put asterisks in front of all the books I hadn't yet read."

"Yes, but you also indicated you would have all the asterisked items read by the time of your examination."

"Yes, I did. I guess I just…ran out of time."

An embarrassed silence fell over the room, and the 18th-century scholar concluded, "Yes, I guess you did."

That was it. Dead in the water. Hanged, drawn, and quartered. I was asked to leave the room while my five executioners conferred. I wandered out into the hallway and flopped onto a sofa, feeling like I'd been run over by a truck, like I'd been mugged—except all my muggers had Ph.Ds (and were therefore all the more vicious). But I knew they were right. I had done horribly: unprepared, flustered, inarticulate. My mind just froze up. Clearly not Ph.D. material. Exposed at last. Didn't make the grade. Couldn't cut the mustard. Just not good enough. They called me back to tell me what I already knew—that I hadn't passed, that I'd have to take both exams again, the written and the oral, "when I felt ready." And also that my dissertation topic—an attempted synthesis of Romanticism and Existentialism, showing the origins of Existentialism in the "Romantic self"—was much too broad, that I'd have to modify it into something "do-able." The 18th-century scholar, who was a bit milder this time, but still skeptical, in the philosophical tradition of his period (his no-nonsense skepticism, so different from my Romantic effusions, was one of the things I most respected about him), put it clearly: "I could no more write a dissertation on your topic than I could jump out the window and fly to Baltimore." I remember feeling a distinct relief at this characterization of the problem, for it reassured me that his reasons for flunking me were not because he felt I'd lied about the books I'd read (which had been my greatest fear during, and after, my interrogation), but because he simply felt my dissertation was impossible. That was fine with me. Impossibility was excusable; lying wasn't. Better to be a dummy than a liar. And so even in my moment of greatest shame, of greatest failure to date, there was a self-congratulatory and irrelevant feeling of vindication: At least I wasn't a bad person.

A week later, I had shut off most of the bedeviling replays and begun writing the first chapter of my dissertation. And over time, although the memory of my shaming before the committee still remains (they passed me the second time around, though even then my performance was less than exemplary), I have come to feel a curious kind of pride in this first evidence of my academic failure, not unlike the pride I came to feel in the aftermath of my horrendous performance—my two horrendous perform-ances—on the typing tests at Doubleday.

This pride continues, in a different but related inflection, in my present academic circumstances, which also fall well short of brilliant. Misplaced though it is, this pride helps me deal with the sense of failure, and points me in another direction, away from academia, and towards—what? Autobiography? My sense of calling as an autobiographer? Or is that just wishful thinking, a rationalization of my perceived failure as being something other than what it is—failure? The wish for there to be a pot of gold at the end of the rainbow of failure—the rainbow that never quite made it, failed to shine, remained only a glimmer?

It was not always thus. There was a time when I was happy to have gotten a tenure-track job at the college where I now teach, when I felt proud to be elevated above my non-tenure-track status at Holy Cross, validated—or as close to validated as I have ever felt—as a "real professor." I no longer feel this way. Although I have published a few articles, and a few book reviews—slim pickings, admittedly, but enough to get tenure—I no longer feel like a "real professor." That feeling has worn off, perhaps due to the contempt bred by familiarity.

I look back with fondness at my first few years here, when my pride arose not as a perverse reaction to the sense of failure, but rather as a natural part of my feeling of success—success in finally having gotten, after four grueling years on the academic job market, a tenure-track job at a private four-year college within an hour of New York City. It could be worse, I told myself; it could be much worse. (And it almost was, considering some of the places I had interviews at.) So for a while I thanked my lucky stars, counted my blessings, and felt proud that I had somehow pulled it off, and had emerged with an assistant professorship in the Greater New York Metropolitan Area.

And I sometimes still feel this way, on my better days. But not usually. Usually I feel about me the heavy pall of academic mediocrity. This feeling is accompanied by a perverse pride, arising perhaps from the fact that I have removed myself from—or just crapped out of—the academic rat race. That I have taken, deliberately or not, another path: the path of the anti-academic academic. A mild-mannered rebel of sorts. The ally of my students (though many of them might not know this, and would be surprised to find out!) against the deadly bureaucracy and empty pedantry of academia. There is pride in such a posture—the pride of opposition, nonconformity, passive resistance—and in the sense of integrity that comes from them. I am aware that it may be a deluded pride—just a cover for the feeling that I am not a "real professor," not a professional, not a serious academic. That I am merely a tenured timeserver.

Thirteen years ago, before I came to my present college, my pride was not of the perverse sort, but was fueled by a genuine sense of accomplishment. This was the "Holy Cross Period." It was also, like all the best times of my life, part of the "Diane Period." In fact, the "Holy Cross Period" was the heart of the "Diane Period"—which is to say, the heart of the heart of my life. The idea of failure was far from my mind at this time. Though not entirely absent; it was not, after all, a tenure-track job that I ended up getting at Holy Cross. I had been told, by the chair of the English Department there, Richard Matlak, that it would last only one year—"two years at the very most." So I had to resume the process of applying for tenure-track jobs almost as soon as I arrived at Holy Cross: a terrible letdown to temper the sense of triumph I carried around with me those first weeks in Worcester. Still, the "Holy Cross Period," especially the first year, was a time of almost uncontainable pride and sense of accomplishment. It is necessary to talk in some detail about this period, because it is, in the larger picture, part of the story of my failure, just as the story of a person's happy marriage—mine, say—can be seen as a golden segment, enduring but finite, in the iron length of loneliness that preceded and follows it.

Almost all of my pride of achievement, I see now, had to do with Diane. With the fact that she was witness to it, partner in it, my confidante and not-so-secret sharer for the whole buildup to the "Holy Cross Period," and then during it, and after it as well, when we moved from Worcester to Long Island and I became a "real professor" (at least for a while). My pride, my sense of achievement and success were all experienced for her, because I knew that she was sharing them. It didn't occur to me at the time, but now it seems clear that's how it was. As I said in the previous chapter, she was my taken-for-granted "horizon of expectation," which gave form and value to my wishes and plans. With her every day took on a sense of drama—or at least of narrative. Literally, because I would tell her my day's doings when I got home, and she would tell me hers. Much of the time I would only half listen to what she said, which of course annoyed her. We developed a shorthand for my poor listening skills (as we did for so much) that was actually a humorous way of shifting blame from me onto her. I would hold my loosened lips between thumbs and forefingers and flap them up and down, in a pantomime of empty speaking. How I miss what I thought was her chatter! How heavy and hard to bear is the silence of returning home to a house without her, evermore! Music on the radio has become more important than ever, as a way to fill the silence and lighten the burden of loneliness. News programs, after all, fill the silence, but do nothing to lighten the burden; only music can do that. Radio and TV, the companions of old age.

As the iron length of my life without Diane gets longer and longer, expanding into the iron future, I go back in memory to happier days, to the golden segment beginning right after Christmas, 1993, at the Modern Language Association's convention in Toronto. Every year, job candidates for academic positions are interviewed at the M.L.A. That year, my first "on the market," I am lucky enough to have four interviews. The last is with Holy Cross, alma mater of my mother's father and brother.

I say "happier days," but for my mother they are not so happy. Three months earlier, in September, she was diagnosed with amyloidosis, a rare, incurable and fatal blood disease. Already she has begun to fail, though she is still walking (that was to change after the chemotherapy—wrongly prescribed—began, when her legs became atrophied, her feet curled and warped), and not yet near the end. Although I know her condition is terminal, it doesn't really register. I cannot understand, or even imagine, what these words mean: "My mother is terminally ill," let alone "She is going to die." She is still very much Mom. (Though this too will change, near the end, when she retreats more and more into her own silent world.) She has always been there, my whole life; how can she not always be there? Along with Diane and Zack, she is one of the three most important people in my life. My father is important in a different way—an intellectual, literary, comic guiding light.

By December of 1993, my mother is no longer as actively important a presence in my life as Diane and Zack; but still, in temperament and sensibility, we are extensions of each other. And she is going to die. And I do not yet believe it. (Have I ever? No, not really.) And neither does she—although she once said to me, shortly after her diagnosis, "I wonder how it will be."

"What do you mean?" I asked, stupidly, knowing exactly what she meant, and wishing I didn't—wishing to keep the thing away, to keep it still vague and impersonal, in the belief that it would, after all, still not come to pass. (It was the same, years later, with Diane's cancer.)

"The end," she said, with the hint of a sick smile, and that note of ironic dread that she had: her way of conveying, with her tone of voice, that distinctive sensibility that we shared, that I had absorbed over the years from her.

"Oh Mom, come on," I said dismissively, veering away from the deep waters she had been unable not to steer us into.

But even now, in December, my mother's terminal illness, still an inconceivable abstraction, is a less pressing matter to me than my four upcoming job interviews at the M.L.A. And I think—or just tell myself—that she would agree. After all, she is as tickled as I am about the Holy Cross interview, inasmuch as she is a decidedly lapsed Catholic, who married a Jew and thought of converting (but was so lapsed that she didn't even do that). And so my interview with Holy Cross, her family's alma mater, becomes a joke between us, a wild coincidence, not to be taken seriously—as all things Catholic are not to be taken seriously by her, by either of us. (This will change as well, at the end, when she asks for a Jesuit priest to be at her funeral service. But even then, true to form, she asks that he be "young and good-looking.")

But then I receive in the mail, before leaving for my interviews, the Holy Cross catalogue, accompanied by a photocopied clipping from *U.S. News and World Report,* showing that Holy Cross is "first-tier", ranked among the top 25 liberal arts colleges in the country. (It comes in 25th, but still, it rates.) The day after Christmas, on the plane from L.A. to Toronto, I go over, in excited preparation, all four catalogues for the schools I'm interviewing with. It is then that the desire for New England, and what I would later come to identify as "the arduous life," begins to form itself in my imagination. It is a desire that has its origins not so much at Exeter as in the few scripts I read in Burbank that were set in New England—representing, diametrically on the map, the farthest-possible wished-for escape from Los Angeles. (Just as my homesickness at Exeter was worsened by my farthest-possible separation from home.) But there is no doubt that the lingering sense of failure experienced in that last New England spring at Exeter is somehow connected with my new-fangled desire now—a desire that, despite our three years in Worcester, was to remain unfulfilled.

But that is getting ahead of myself. On the plane to Toronto, the desire for Holy Cross and New England that I am beginning to feel takes the form not of an unfulfilled desire, but of a recognition: the recognition of a new life, a new kind of life. And not just an abstract recognition—I have had that for years, connected with the desire to escape the only place I have ever called home: an unformed desire to escape the placid, sterile streets of the

Palisades, the streets of my childhood, with their familiar, contrived Spanish and Indian names, like Toyopa, Chautauqua, Ocampo, Almaloya, Corona Del Mar. My desire takes the form now, in Toronto (another Indian name, but so different, so utterly other, severe and frozen), of a more concrete response—my response to the cold northern city. To the steam coming from its gray smokestacks and rooftops, seen from the windows of the penthouse pool in the hotel where we are staying. To the frozen northern lake (Ontario). To the frigid wind, bracing and breathtaking. To the winter clothing, with the women's cold, keen faces peeking out from furry hoods and woolen caps—their eyes bright and darting and vital in the cold air, interested and alive. It is the vision of a new life, so strange and suddenly so attractive to me, a new life of striving and achieving in the cold north—a whole new possible way of living, this life of cold winters, under a gray or freezing-blue sky, with the stakes of life ratcheted up a notch or two. The heart beating faster in the cold air; the sense that things somehow matter more in the press of the cold, in the bustle of the great northern city. I remember sitting in a hotel mezzanine, waiting for one of my interviews, looking out a wide plate-glass window onto the frozen lake, with ice floes in it—ice floes in a lake! I have never seen such a thing before, with the sun glowing feebly through the gray winter cloud-cover. And I suddenly know that I want all of this. I am ready. Let it begin.

My Holy Cross interview is the last of the four, and I nail it. There are three members of the English Department interviewing me that morning in a hotel room (the Delta Chelsea—how could I forget?): the chair, Rich Matlak, a Wordsworth scholar; a poet, Robert Cording; and a Shakespearean, Helen Whall—an attractive blonde with a strong Boston accent (Dorchester, I later learn). With Matlak I talk about Wordsworth (I am finishing a dissertation on Byron and Wordsworth). With Whall I talk about movies: She wants to know what movies I like, and if I have recommended any scripts in my reading jobs that have been made into movies. Cording, the poet, is quiet, listening attentively. There is much laughter all around. I feel I can do no wrong. From the start of the interview I hit the ground running and just keep going, full steam ahead. The time—a half-hour? forty-five minutes? an hour, even?—passes in an exhilarating blur, and I leave the hotel room walking on air, my heart aflutter with a secret overflowing joy as I float past the next candidate, waiting in the hallway as I had done, my head spinning with the excitement of it all, and the sense of my small but real triumph. Who knows if I will get the job? That doesn't matter right now. What matters is that I have nailed the interview. I know I couldn't have done any better. This new life, the vision of a new life for all of us, comes a little bit closer to realization that day. I can taste it in the frozen, triumphal air.

That afternoon, we take Zack to the Toronto Science Museum. A long trip out into the suburbs by subway, then bus, under an overcast sky. But the gray winter sky isn't bad, it's good. It is, for me on this day, a sky of happiness and triumph; it makes everything more special, more memorable. Having grown up in the land of perennial sunshine, I have never minded overcast days; in fact I have often preferred them, especially for memorable events. ("Men have oftener suffered from the mockery of a place too smiling for their reason than from the oppression of surroundings over-sadly tinged"—Hardy.) Gray skies have always heightened my feelings of happiness when I'm happy, and spoken of happiness, or pointed the way to it, when I am sad.

The overcast winter sky on this memorable Toronto day of the nailed Holy Cross interview, and the cold, and the long expedition on unfamiliar public transportation out into the strange, frozen suburbs of the great Northern city—all are part of the aura of triumph, the sense of making an incursion, taking the first real step into a new and devoutly-wished-for life. The already-gilded highlights of the Holy Cross interview, and the haze of excitement in which they float, provide the emotional background of the exhibits I see that day at the museum. But actually, that gets it backwards: It is the Holy Cross interview that I am really seeing at the museum, and the museum exhibits are merely the context and setting of the remembered interview. All those exhibits have now receded back into a memorial haze. Except for one: a Rube Goldberg-like contraption, antique and circus-looking, resembling a *New Yorker* cover by the artist Joseph Low—a whimsical construction of levers and ramps and wheels for balls to travel along, which stands in the front lobby of the museum, which our seven-year-old finds endlessly fascinating to observe in action, and which is pleasing to let my mind play over.

But as I stand with Zack before the machine, what my mind is really playing over is the thrumming sense of a new life just that day beginning—or not even beginning yet, but about to begin—"bidding fair to begin," to use the antique diction appropriate to the contraption. A new life glimpsed and approaching in the far distance, under the overcast sky of the north. A life of heightened meaning, pursuit, and achievement—of what Wordsworth called "effort, and expectation, and desire."

As it happened, I didn't get the job. I learned this sometime in early February, when I called Rich Matlak to let him know I had a campus interview at one of the other colleges I'd interviewed with in Toronto, and to find out where I stood with Holy Cross, in case I should receive a job offer from the other school (I didn't). Kindly and regretfully, he informed me that I didn't make the second cut. He said he "wished it had gone otherwise." I hung up the phone feeling oddly buoyed by his words. Despite my bitter disappointment, it was also gratifying, and fuel for future contemplations, to know that my high hopes for Holy Cross had not gone unreciprocated. He "wished it had gone otherwise," and I believed him. A connection was made in that hotel room on that memorable day in Toronto.

It was that connection—unfruitful, apparently, but not illusory, and not quite finished, either, I sensed (though I also told

myself this was probably just wishful thinking)—that my mind
continued to play over during the next weeks and months. There
were a few more job interviews, including one at an art college,
The Museum School, in Boston. A trip back there in March gave
me a taste of late winter/early spring in New England, which I
hadn't experienced for 20 years. Mostly it was late winter, rainy
and cold. I stayed over the weekend to save the school money
on the plane ticket they'd bought for me. Immediately after the
interview, I learned from the search committee chair that I hadn't
gotten the job. (This was a gross violation of protocol, said Peter
Manning, my dissertation director, and old friend from Berkeley
days; he was furious when he heard about it.) But I had to go out
to dinner anyway with her and her philosopher husband. I tried
to be philosophical, too, and we talked about Stanley Cavell, the
saxophone-playing Harvard philosopher.

Saturday, the day after the interview, was a splendorous spring
day. I walked down Brattle Street in Cambridge, past Longfellow's old mansion, butter-yellow in the pellucid Harvard
sunshine. I suddenly recognized it again after all these years, that
special light, the cleansed New England light and air that etch in
sharp relief every object they touch. There is no light like it. The
light of poets and philosophers, the light of the blessed denizens
of Harvard, the princes of the world—a world from which I was
forever excluded. And no more so than that day, that beautiful
New England day in early spring, after which I had to return to
the land of smog and undistinguished light. Despite my conclu-
sive rejection by Harvard, I had somehow never stopped aspiring
to it—the Harvard of my mind, anyway, holding it as an emblem
and a value, as part of my ideal world. To walk in the warm sun
on Brattle Street was to revive once again that old painful fantasy,
that adolescent dream which was not all a dream, since here I was,
20 years later, having just interviewed for a teaching job across
the river, east of Eden. And although I was, apparently, rejected
once again, there I still was, as if in waiting for something, some
sort of pledge that it was not all over between me and Harvard,

me and Boston, me and New England. Despite my history of rejection and disappointment in that city (which were two of the things that made me attracted to it), I could still enjoy the fine light and air of that early spring day. Indeed, the morning took on a poignant, lyrical, elegiac quality precisely because of that disappointment and rejection. I could appreciate its beauty all the more because I was debarred from living under what Wordsworth would call its "more habitual sway."

The following Monday, back at MGM in Santa Monica (where I had been working since the previous fall), I thought over these things: memories of early spring in Boston; the regretful Rich Matlak at Holy Cross, and that whole drama of great expectations and disappointment; the life and "light that never was, on sea or land." (Wordsworth again, "Peele Castle." This time he's talking about the ideal, imaginary light in a painting—which is what the New England light was to me.) But these were not bitter memories and imaginings, these musings that I had—they were not bitter at all, even though they had not come to fruition. They were somehow sweet and comforting, despite the disappointment. (Was there even something comforting about the disappointment?) Wordsworth would have understood. These memories and imaginings were the bearers of hope—hope disappointed, perhaps even banished; but still alive, despite rejection and debarment. ("Not without hope we suffer and we mourn"—"Peele Castle" again.)

That didn't mean I still had any hope for those jobs, the Museum School job or the Holy Cross job. I had been told, in no uncertain terms, that I was no longer a candidate for either of them. So where did the hope come from? To what was it directed? It came from Toronto, and the ice floes in the lake, and the gray winter skies; and also the sunshine on Brattle Street, and Longfellow's butter-yellow mansion (the same color as Mr. Fish's house at Exeter, with the cannon and balls out front). And it was directed at my new life—our new life, our "northern life," which did not yet exist, but which had begun to form itself, vaguely and insistently, in my mind. This hope was both geographical and personal, deriving from places I had been to and desires nourished there—desires prompted by ambitions connected with those places. They had not panned out, those ambitions, but the hopes and desires had not been wiped out, either. They still hovered in my mind's eye, under the gray northern winter sky, and in the light of Brattle Street.

They hovered most insistently, for some reason, during my lunchtime laps in the MGM swimming pool. I was usually the only person in the pool. It was a shallow lap pool, waist-deep, probably so they would not have to pay for a life guard on the premises. There was a brick-glass skylight running the length of the pool. And because this was L.A., and not Toronto or Boston, the sun was almost always shining through the skylight. But that was fine with me. I liked to flip over during my laps and look up at the skylight while doing the backstroke. And what I saw, when I did this, was not just the refracted light coming through the brick glass; it was also the faces of my Holy Cross interviewers, and the frozen gray Toronto skyline, seen from the windows of the penthouse pool of our hotel, belching winter steam from its smokestacks and rooftops; and Longfellow's butter-yellow mansion in the early spring sunlight. What I saw were the scenes of my desires—like my "scenes of reading"—which continued to hover around me in the chlorinated air.

And meanwhile, during all of this, my mother was slowly dying at home, a few miles away. This too was part of my "scene of reading" at MGM—though one that I pushed to the back of my mind. It was not a scene to be lingered over, or "contemplated about." It was that rarest of all things in my life—the unimaginable.

In May of 1994 I had my last (failed) interview, up at Stanford—a short-term, non tenure-track instructorship, but still, it was Stanford. I blew it by being very nervous at the interview, which was in a small office, packed with all sorts of professors. I mentioned "the flaws in my dissertation," thinking this would be taken as a disarming show of intellectual honesty, but instead it was taken as the sign of a loser. The job went to someone else.

Back at MGM, the readers' offices were moved from upper-story rooms, with a view of the ocean, and planes taking off from Santa Monica Airport, to basement rooms, with a view of an interior hallway. But actually, I did not really mind the move, even though my basement office was dark and claustrophobic; or if I did mind it, my displeasure didn't last very long. Just before Memorial Day, I got a call from Peter Manning, who had received an email from Rich Matlak (they were fellow-Wordsworthians), asking if I was still available—and, if I was, asking Peter to inform me that I was "invited" to apply for a one-year sabbatical replacement job at Holy Cross. If I did apply, Matlak told Peter, "my application would be taken seriously." I didn't need to be asked twice.

The next day I Fedexed my application letter, and the window-less basement room was instantly transformed from a dark place of exile into a private, even cozy "scene of great expectations." The scenes of hope, desire, and ambition that the scripts I was reading evoked now took on an even more promising coloring. And these scenes were not just limited to scripts. An issue of *National Geographic*, which Zack had received a gift subscription to, featured a photo essay on Boston, accompanied by a map of the Eastern seabord from Boston to D.C., and an article on the growing Boston–New York–Philadelphia–Baltimore–D.C. "megalopolis." The map and photo spread, including shots of be-gowned princes and princesses of Harvard at graduation, and the Boston skyline at sunset, with the requisite white and red trails of car lights wending homeward—a photo evocative, comforting, and corny, as sunset photos in *National Geographic* tend to be—these photos and map went up on my wall in the dark basement room, to fuel my "efforts, expectations, and desires" in the days and weeks to come, and to provide their visible counterpart.

And so the weeks went by, without another word from Holy

Cross. Hope, which I had been deliberately (and unsuccessfully) attempting to suppress ever since I sent off the second job letter, now began to wane. Still, I told myself, surely I had a better chance than most of the other applicants this time, having been "invited" to apply. But I knew the competition was intense, even for one-year positions. I would not fool myself. I was ready for the long roller-coaster ride of my first year on the academic job market to be over. I was not complaining. I had come close several times.

Then, one morning at the end of June—June 29, to be exact—the phone call came. I had been wondering, in the not-so-back of my mind, when and how it would come. And now here it was: a message on my voice-mail, when I came into my dark office that morning, from Rich Matlak, asking me to call him, and leaving his number at Holy Cross. That's all. A man of few words. But that was all it took to set my heart racing. The message was rather curt, and his voice sounded serious and sober. Not a voice of celebration or congratulation; a voice once more of regret, of "wishing it had gone otherwise." I heard those words again in my head as my heart kept racing, and I played out in my mind how our second phone conversation would go. It would go much like the first. He would be kind and regretful. He would say, again, the sad but soothing words of rejection. And I would again hang up feeling crestfallen, yet vaguely buoyed. Probably even more disappointed this time, since my hopes, despite the efforts to restrain them, had risen even higher than before, because of all that had come between. I was prepared for all of this. The map and photos I had put on the wall seemed to mock my hopes, though they were still emblems of my desire. I decided to take them down after the phone call.

But I didn't just take them down—I took them with me to Worcester, MA, along with my wife and son. Because the call was not a rejection call. When I called him back, and the department secretary put me through to him, Rich Matlak said, in a tone of restrained excitement and pleasure, "Josh, we'd like to offer you the job." The rest of the conversation took place in a delirious haze. I could not contain my happiness, nor did I want to—not that day, nor the next, nor for weeks to come, as we prepared to move across the country, from L.A. to Worcester (again, that diagonal trip from coast to coast, from southern California to New England, reminiscent of Exeter days); leaving the apartment we'd lived in for the past 12 years, the city where I grew up, where Diane and I met and got married, where our son was born.

And where my mother was dying, and I was leaving her. We were all leaving her; her only grandchild was going, too. From her point of view, it must have seemed as if we were taking what was left of her life with us. A month or two after we left, she began to have trouble walking. And when I flew from Boston to Minnesota that November, to be with her and my father for an evaluation at the Mayo Clinic, I could see at once, as they brought her off the plane in a wheelchair, that she was dying for real. I hadn't seen it before, but now I did, all at once, clearly. She had gotten much worse in the two and a half months since I had last seen her. She was pale, and shockingly thin. She smiled broadly—and all the more pathetically—when she saw me waiting at the gate. I made myself smile back at her, at a distance, as they wheeled her down the ramp, when what I really wanted to do was yell "Mom!" and run crying into her arms. I could see there was no way out for her now. The evaluation by the amyloidosis specialist at the Mayo Clinic confirmed this.

But that is another story, our week at the Mayo clinic, when my mother saw Canada geese for the last time. She always loved the sight and sound of them flying overhead. And now, living on Long Island, a place permanently occupied by armies of Canada geese, I can never hear them passing overhead without thinking of her. And of Diane, too—always of Diane. Because whenever she saw them, she would say softly, "Hi, Mom."

The college where I now teach used to have lots of Canada geese, waddling and pooping on the paths and front lawn, facing the river. But the grounds crew got a border collie, Barbara, to chase them across the river to the arboretum, where they have occupied the great front lawn there. My college is in a lovely setting, which compensates a little for the fact that it is a mediocre school.

How did I end up here? A child of privilege, an honors and high-honors graduate of Exeter and Berkeley, who published his first novel at 26—how did I end up at a commuter college on Long Island? Surely I was meant for something better? A person of my abilities, qualifications, great expectations? Surely there is some mistake? Surely the mistake will soon be rectified, and I will find my proper place—if not the Ivy League, for I have no illusions there, then at least a solidly second-tier school, a Cal State, or a Penn State, or a Florida State. How did I fall so far from what might have been expected? Was it because I didn't get into Harvard? Was that the beginning of my slippery slope? Or because I waited too long—10 years—to go to grad school? Or because I went to USC, which was then a second-tier school? Or because my dissertation—on Byron's poetic relation to Wordsworth—was not trendy, theoretical, or brilliant enough? (Or not brilliant at all, if the truth be told.) Who knows, and who cares?

I try not to think about these things, but when I do find myself thinking about them anyway, I remind myself that I am lucky to have found a tenure-track job at all. I know of more than a few who didn't—who never completed their dissertations, or who gave up the grueling job search, or went from one poorly paid adjunct position to another, or got a sabbatical-replacement job, or more than one, but nothing more. When I think of them—my partners in failure, my doubles, my brothers (and sisters)—the burden of disillusionment is lightened, not so much by a familiar, specious feeling of self-congratulation, as by a superstitious gratitude, an amazed thankfulness that the Sword of Damocles has not fallen (yet), that I have been spared.

For what? For this. For my little project of self-evisceration. Which would not be possible if I were at a better school, where I would be expected to publish a steady flow of scholarly articles and books, or short stories, or novels. No, I am where I need to be, to do what I need to do. And for this, I am grateful.

Is this merely a rationalization? Not really. After all, if I were at a better school, I would almost certainly not have gotten tenure. Such a failure would have been much worse—more traumatic, painful, uprooting, for all of us—and would probably have meant the end of my academic career. But it would also have been great grist for the mill. It would have been a genuine academic failure, instead of this mere (though pervasive) *sense* of failure. It might have produced a more gripping account, a dramatic tale of academic ruthlessness, back-stabbing, victimization. The story of one expelled from the ivory tower, rather than continuing to live—however uneasily—within it.

But it should be clear by now that this is an account of an "internal" failure, more than an "external" one—an account, as I have often put it, of the "sense of failure," even the conviction of failure, rather than a documentation of actual failures. You might even consider it a failed account of failure. What better example of failure than that? In any case, the failure that I have been given—as a gift, so to speak—is not the failure of academic rejection or expulsion, but inclusion in a community of academic mediocrity. A place in which I feel at home. In which I feel I belong—a "humble dwelling, but my own," to paraphrase Herr Settembrini once again. Its humbleness and obscurity have freed me up to do what I want: to teach what I want, to write what I want. It is a refuge of sorts, which gives me freedom to "contemplate about" whatever comes to me. My college, I now see, is like my bathroom in the old house in Pacific Palisades, where plans were made, and events pondered, in the humble, protected freedom of the toilet, where the stinking vapors mixed with my contemplational dreaminess to produce the heady, individual aroma of selfhood. I have rediscovered, in my college, from which I will probably never escape—from which I do not, really, even *want* to escape—the re-creation of my cherished childhood bathroom, a place of retreat, repair, thoughtfulness, peace. It may be that the actual products of my present retreat turn out to be no better than the excretions of yore. That is not for me to decide. But if my book, like my academic career, turns out to be crap, I hope that it can serve as fertilizer for others that will be nutritive and life-giving, and maybe even yield some pretty little flowers: *The Flowers of Failure*.

11

My Failure as a Husband

I said earlier that feelings of guilt and remorse did not have a place in my life with Diane—with one glaring exception. That was an internet flirtation—more than a flirtation, really: a romance, on my end at least—with an old girlfriend, which went on for several years, near the end of Diane's life. I'll call her Cindy. (She was the same one who'd dumped me 20 years earlier.) Diane found out about it, and asked me, repeatedly, to end it. I promised her that I would, but I didn't—not until the final year of her life. (And even then, not completely.) I would go for a few months without contacting Cindy; but inevitably, the temptation and the high of Instant Messaging with her, the chimes that sounded when she sent me a message, were too much for me to resist, and I would eventually end up IM-ing her, or sending her an email, and the cycle would begin all over again.

I sometimes wonder whether the pain I gave Diane by continuing this relationship hastened (or maybe even caused?) the recurrence of her cancer. The idea seems not so crazy if you believe in biofeedback, as Diane did. (And because she did, I do, too.) I broke the bond of love and trust that had always existed between us, and such a thing could not be without consequences. On the other hand, to believe that those consequences were the recurrence of her illness, and then her death, seems to me not only monstrously self-centered, but almost biblical as well, and my moral beliefs are not of that sort. (Though the masochism of guilt that goes with such an idea of punishment is right up my alley.)

But the consequences of my infidelity—or my betrayal, to use Diane's word, which is a better one—are not what I want to focus on here. In the last year of her life, after the second surgery, which revealed that the metastasis was inoperable, she forgave me. She stopped asking me whether I had broken it off with Cindy. She even approached Cindy at a party and was cordial to her (as Cindy told me later, in an Instant Message). The thought of Diane's forgiveness—her forgiveness of both of us—fills me not so much with shame as with more love of her: a proud sort of love, much stronger than mere admiration, though related to it. She did what I don't know if I could do, if I were in her place: she made things right with her rival—her perceived rival, that is. Because even in the intensest throes of our virtual affair, Cindy was no rival to Diane. But Diane made things right with her anyway, before she exited the stage—30 years too soon, and leaving a good smell behind. No grudges, no bitterness, no resentment. A class act, all the way. And to think that I used to find fault with her for being prone to resentment! Whereas I myself was all too prone to betrayal. I failed to be, for her, what I should have been, to do what I should have done—and, more to the point, not to do what I shouldn't have done.

It didn't seem like a failure at the time. Quite the opposite. It felt like an affirmation, a rebellious affirmation of passion, sexuality, youth (at 46!), health (mine) as opposed to illness (hers). And more than anything else, the discovery of a secret life—a tremendously exciting secret life. The excitement lay largely in the secrecy, but also in the new sense of myself gained from having a secret life, kept hidden from my mate, from whom

I'd never hidden anything important before. Diane knew every-thing about me, including all the lowly, unseemly bodily details that transpire during an intimate life together: my prolonged childhood bedwetting (since she was almost five years older than I, one of her favorite lines was: "I was [slow dancing, kissing boys, tripping, having sex, having sex while tripping!—you fill in the blank] when you were still wetting the bed"), my eccentric bathroom habits, my masturbation, my noisome flatu-lence (which I reveled in, like a Neanderthal). In the face of such domesticated knowledge, the secret of an affair—even just a "virtual" affair—was irresistible; as was its excitement, its strange excitement, after all the taken-for-granted familiarities of married life.

I still remember that first electrical shock of adultery: the shock of feeling, all anew, the power of sex, which had grown dormant in the routines of matrimony, and how helpless I was to resist it. I remember also—verbatim—the Instant Messenger dialogue we had that set me off:

CINDY (chime): I was thinking about you.
ME (chime): And what were you thinking?
CINDY (chime): I was thinking about sex.

That was it. Just three short lines, and I was hooked. My heart was thumping like crazy, as it hadn't in years. (Maybe never before.) My hands were trembling so that I couldn't type. Trium-phantly, Cindy mocked my typos. The power of a woman. I was putty in her hands. In the space of a few moments—three lines of text, three chimes—I had become unfaithful to Diane. I had crossed over the line, from fidelity to infidelity. It didn't matter that it was "virtual" infidelity. A breach had been opened, not just in cyberspace, but extending into my real life, our real life, of almost 20 years together. Into that breach I now fell—willingly, even eagerly. I wanted to fall. I wanted to know what it felt like to fall, to cross over, to have an affair.

For many years, since before Diane and I were even married, I had been fantasizing about another woman. About what it would be like to feel another woman's skin. To smell another woman's smell. To hear another woman's sounds. To taste her taste. I had dipped my toe in the waters of flirtation—always in Diane's absence—a number of times, but had gone no further than that. A kiss in the bathroom at a party in New York (Diane was back in L.A., pregnant). A late-night walk around the block while Diane was asleep, when I met a woman I'd noticed before, who lived down the street. We went for a drink, and I kissed her goodnight at her door. Flirtatious conversations and lunches with women in graduate school, at the studios where I worked, and then with a graduate student (not mine) when I was a new professor. I told Diane about some of these women, but not all. Since none of them became physical (except for those two restrained kisses), I figured that telling her about the others would only have hurt her, without adding anything new to her knowledge of my weakness. Though now I think I should have told her, since to have withheld even such minor lapses from her, now that she is dead, was an act of deception that can never be made up.

But Cindy was no minor lapse. She had been my last and most serious romance before I met Diane. She was beautiful (and still is)—the most beautiful woman I had ever been with. I was infatuated. The less emotionally accessible she became to me—and emotional inaccessibility was her speciality, her protective camouflage—the more infatuated I became. It took her giving me the cold shoulder when I flew back to New York after Christmas of 1980—watching TV with her full-length cotton nightie on, not talking—for me to finally get the message. I left her in a petulant huff, and a month later I met Diane. But it took a while longer for me to work Cindy out of my system—and even then, not completely. There was unfinished business between us, which didn't get finished until Diane died.

☙

I remember writing a friendly letter to Cindy the April after I'd met Diane, and getting a friendly reply. Then I called her (was this after the letter? I think so), still infatuated, and mentioned, in the course of our conversation, how "devoted" Diane was. "Devotion," Cindy instantly dubbed her. Well, what did I expect? What would have been my response if she'd flaunted her new boyfriend at me?

After those two exchanges, there was nothing more between us for years. I would hear about her from time to time through our mutual friends in New York, Miles and Sarah. She had a ten-year relationship with a handsome, nice guy—a sound editor, which she became, too—but that ended. There was a terrible sadness, too: the loss of their child, which she'd carried almost to term. Hearing about this stirred things up a bit for me. The thought of Cindy as a mother, with a mother's vulnerabilities (strength had always been her thing, not vulnerability; I was the vulnerable one)—and then to suffer a loss like that. I guess it humanized her for me. But that is putting it too abstractly. I felt sorry for her. She had suffered. It must have been horrible, to go through what she went through; and even though she would never show it, I knew she had suffered, and I felt sorry for her. I also felt superior to her, in my characteristic, less-than-admirable way. I was married, and a parent; she was neither. She had made me suffer, way back when, but I had prevailed. She had been punished.

Did I really see it that way? Was I still so hurt and bitter? (Talk about resentful!) Did I really harbor such hateful feelings? Not consciously; and I never would have described my feelings that way, not even to myself. But like them or not, they were there, fueling my smugness and self-satisfaction where Cindy was concerned.

These weren't the only feelings I had for her, though. There was still that unfinished business between us. (Unfinished at least "in my mind," as Clint would say.) There was still her beauty, the memory of her beauty. And the memory of those few fevered moments on the floor, in my car, in the woods in the mountains, and against the railing of the Venice pier the night before she flew back to New York. But her sexual transport—unlike Diane's—was a thing separate and apart from emotional access, which I was never granted. Maybe that was why our sexual connection, though brief, was so intense: it was the only connection we had.

These were not details I shared with Diane, of course—though I had told her all about the unhappy aspects of our relationship. She had met Cindy several times in New York, and didn't like her. She described her as "swooping down" on us. She was put off by her loudness, her raucous laugh, and her drinking. All of this was true. Cindy was louder than she had been, and drank more than she used to, years ago. She had reason to drink, I explained; but I wasn't so sure about the loudness, other than that it went along with the drinking (though she had the raucous laugh even when she didn't drink). Insecurity? Aggression? The wish merely to be noticed? But how could she not be noticed? She was still beautiful, even Diane acknowledged that. Her striking features—nose (ever so slightly hooked), eyes (hazel, slightly drooping), mouth (a little buck-toothed), cheekbones (yes!)—had softened with age, and she kept herself in good physical shape. (She demonstrated this once by wrestling with Zack.) And she had the most gorgeous skin I had ever beheld, soft and golden and flawless. Yes, I still noticed. She was as beautiful as ever—and made even more so, to me, by the knowledge of her sad story.

But she also knew how to have fun, Cindy did, especially with the kids she didn't have. The first Thanksgiving after we'd moved to Massachusetts, we came down to New York and Cindy arranged for a bunch of us with kids to watch the Macy's parade from her office in the Brill Building. I felt a little tug then, seeing how much she enjoyed making the kids happy. Zack was more interested in the sound-editing equipment than the parade, and she gave him a demonstration. I felt a complicated twinge there too, and not just for her sake. I remembered I'd once told her, on an impulse, that I wanted to have a child with her, and she reacted with embarrassment. Watching Cindy and Zack, I wondered about the child we might—or might not—have had. The fact that she clearly had not wanted a child with me (or probably with anyone, at that time in her life) escaped me for the moment, and I wondered if that child would have been anything like Zack. I wondered if she was wondering that, too.

A couple of months later, at the end of January, we were down in New York again, this time for the Burns Night party that Miles and Sarah gave every year. I was feeling very light-headed that night. There was much to feel light-headed about—not all of it good, though all of it brought a sense of drama, change, high-stakes excitement. (For my mother, the highest of stakes. Back in L.A., she was seriously ill with the blood disease from which she would die the following June.) The night of the Burns party, I had drunk enough to feel even higher than usual. It was always a high to come to New York, and our relative proximity now to the city was yet another confirmation of the ratcheting-up of our lives since we'd moved from L.A. It seemed to me that I had only now finally left home, once and for all. The guilty knowledge that my mother lay bedridden and slowly dying back home in L.A.—and that she had really only begun to die, in a sense, after we had moved away—gave our life a new gravity and irrevocability. Life without a safety net. It was both scary and thrilling. It was, finally, full adulthood. (Ten years later, when it had all passed with Diane's death, I would come to call this time of my life—our three years in Worcester—the "height" of my "Major Period.")

At some point in the evening I found myself alone with Cindy in the elevator, headed down to the liquor store across West 86th Street to buy more wine. I looked at her, she looked at me, and we met in an embrace. My ears were ringing. Did I say something to her, something drunkenly romantic like "I've always loved you" or "I've never stopped loving you"? I think I did. Probably, knowing me, I would have had to say something. As if I had to account for my actions. As if desire needed a justification. (As if there could have been a justification.) Then the elevator doors opened and we were rushing across the street in the cold. We bought the wine and rushed back upstairs again. We didn't want to be gone too long, or people—meaning Diane—would start to wonder. Perhaps she had already started to wonder. Diane and I didn't make love that night, as we usually did when we came to New York. Instead, as she slept beside me in her mother's bed (her mother always slept on the couch in the living room when we came to visit), I replayed that embrace in the elevator. I didn't feel too great; in fact, I felt a little queasy. And the fact that her mother had given up her bed so that I, an adulterer in my heart, could not make love to her daughter in it, didn't make me feel any better.

If this was all part of our new life without a safety net, falling—a little fall, anyway—was part of the deal. That didn't make me feel any better, either.

I mention all this as preface to the "big fall" of 2000 (in both senses). My feelings for Cindy, whatever they were—lustful, yearning, fantastical, all of these—were nothing like the "soul-love" I had with Diane; but then it was their relative superficiality that gave those feelings their power over my imagination. And superficial though they were, they had never really died; they had just been buried inside, where they were now sprouting again, like mushrooms in the dark. This darkness, and its fruits, were thrilling to me, a timid, sensitive, fickle creature of fantasy. Whenever I would tell myself that Diane was a better person than Cindy; that I must not betray her; that I couldn't risk losing the life we had built together; that I was also betraying Zack (the thought of his precarious sexual innocence—he was about to turn 13—was especially poignant to me)—none of what I told myself availed to stop my daily Instant Messages to Cindy. The sound of the chimes announcing each message, though by now familiar, was still as irresistible as the first time, on that day in October. In fact, the sound took me back every time to that first time, and the forbidden excitement of what we were doing. When Diane was home, of course, I shut off the chimes. But even then I could not refrain from sending messages to Cindy. I hid the AIM window at the bottom of the screen and seemingly focused my attention on my school email, keeping one eye at all times on the menu bar, waiting for the little rectangle with Cindy's new message in it to start flashing blue, my heart pounding the whole time.

It went on like this for the better part of three months. But our affair was not limited to "virtual" meetings. Several times I took the train into the city to have lunch with her, under cover of having lunch with Miles, in whose office Cindy (conveniently) now worked. This set-up was why I could count on her being online all day, five days a week. My new secret life as a virtual adulterer was, in that sense, a by-product—one of millions, I'm sure—of the "communications revolution" created by the Internet. My experience of the possibilities,the sexual possibilities, of this new medium was also part of my excitement. Not that I was interested in trying this with someone I didn't know; that would have struck me as creepy. (The fact that I was being a creep to Diane didn't even occur to me. Unfaithful, yes; creep, no. My self-deception here enabled me to congratulate myself once again on the sins I wasn't committing, while conveniently passing over those that I was.) It wasn't the anonymity of Internet sex that I was after; it was the secrecy and curious intimacy of it. How could you be intimate with someone you didn't know? The fact that Cindy and I had been lovers made it even more exciting. As for the secrecy—after 20 years of living together, there seemed to be no secrets left between my soul mate and me. None, that is, except this.

Cindy was never explicitly sexual in her messages to me (except in that first one, never to be repeated), and not really even implicitly sexual, except in the fact that she did not rebuff me. The sex on my end was highly romantic: emotional fantasies of kissing her, nostalgic evocations of our passionate times together.

These memories were much more romantic than they ever had been in reality. But the easy availability of romanticized "virtual sex" with my ex-girlfriend wasn't enough for me (and was made even more exciting by the possibility that it might not remain "virtual"), so I came to Miles's office a few times and took her to lunch.

I'd had lunch with them once already, innocently enough, before the affair started. I had sent an Instant Message to Miles, who then phoned and, in the course of our conversation, mentioned that Cindy was working for him. We arranged to have lunch, and Cindy came, too. After lunch, Miles went back to the office, but Cindy stayed and we talked for a while. On the train back to Long Island, replaying the lunch in my mind, I remember being struck by the fact that even though Diane had finished a hellishly aggressive course of cancer treatment only four months earlier (radical mastectomy; chemotherapy with Adriamycin, the dreaded "Red Devil," among other poisons; then radiation), hardly any questions were asked about how she was doing. I remembered her being a little put out with Miles and Sarah for not calling more often, and this now seemed justified. On the other hand, Miles was an old friend of mine. I liked his easy-going, thoughtful tolerance, and his ironic humor. But I do remember being somewhat disappointed by our lunch—and by Cindy as well. She'd given up a successful career as a sound editor to take an office job, working for her friend. I was aware that my self-congratulatory judgmentalness about her was now returning; but why bother to challenge it?

Soon after this, I went to a conference in Boston, and for a couple of weeks after I got back I didn't think much about Cindy. Our meeting seemed to have put her in her place again, back in my past, where my conscience told me she belonged.

Because of my teaching schedule that fall, I had more time on my hands than usual. After finishing my school email one day I found myself drifting into Instant Messager, just out of curiosity. But it wasn't Miles I was curious about, and it wasn't him I sent an Instant Message to. Cindy was glad to hear from me. She said she hadn't heard from me for a few weeks. And then, those three short, life-changing lines:

CINDY: I was thinking about you.
ME: And what were you thinking?
CINDY: I was thinking about sex.

"Life-changing"? It seems yet another betrayal of Diane to call them that. "Life-changing" was getting the job at Holy Cross, and moving from L.A. to Worcester, and then getting the tenure-track job on Long Island, and moving there. "Life-changing" was my mother's illness and death. And more than anything, "life-changing" was meeting and falling in love with Diane, and making a life with her, and having Zack. The life that was changed by these personally momentous events was our shared life, 20 years in the making. A life of fullness, and purpose, and commitment, and love. The changes undergone in that life together were embraced by both of us, in pursuit of our continuing, evolving life together. The circumstances and locations of that shared life might alter, but its foundations never would.

But a breach had now opened in that life—a breach that I had created, and fallen willingly into, head over heels. Another life, a parallel life. As I saw it, or wanted to see it, this secret, "virtual" life was something entirely different and separate from my shared life with Diane. Of course, it wasn't really a life at all, as the "virtual" suggests. It was a possible life—an *imagined* possible life. A fantasized life. Cindy knew this much better than I. She called me "Mr. Fantasy." Her role in the affair, it seemed—or at least her preference—was either to deflate or ignore my fantasies; and also, when we had been discovered, but I could not stop writing to her, to voice a half-hearted moral conscience to balance my lack of one.

Not only did I not stop writing to Cindy after Diane found

out and made me promise to stop, but I occasionally would propose—with a manic mixture of fantasy, facetiousness, and romantic wishfullness—ways for us to meet, such as a golf outing, or a swim at the beach (Cindy was athletic; Diane wasn't). These proposals were met with incredulous reproach: "An actual *meeting*? Are you kidding?" The response was expected, and secretly made me feel a little relieved. I'm not sure what I would have done if she'd agreed to meet. Probably chickened out. After all, my cover of lunches with Miles had now been blown. What excuse for my absence in the middle of the day would I give Diane, if she asked? Even if I had engineered a way for Cindy and me to meet (though I had never been able, up until then, to maintain even the simplest of lies), I almost certainly would have spent the entire time plagued by guilt, remorse, and fear. No doubt Cindy foresaw this Hobson's Choice, and preempted it by her refusal, which was carried out on moral as well as practical grounds. She had strict ideas about right and wrong, taught to her by her English mother and grandmother.

So why, if she was so "moral" (as I sometimes teased her for being, feeling ashamed and sleazy as I did so, but also knowing that I was playing a role—the role of the "shameless lover," the man carried away by passion—which excited me), why then did she keep writing back to me? Why did she never leave a message or email unanswered? This was the question Diane asked when she threatened to call Cindy (her number was in my address book). I begged her not to. I said it was all my fault, that it had been my idea, that Cindy was just acquiescing to me, that she was never an initiator of our exchanges. (Which was true.) And that I would tell her it was over. (Which it wasn't, and which I didn't.)

Why? Why couldn't I just stop writing her for good? My shrink said it was an addiction, and no doubt this was true. The excitement I got from sending Instant Messages to Cindy—and, particularly, receiving them from her—was a drug-like rush I hadn't felt in years, if ever. But however exciting our messages were to me, there was always something self-conscious in my reaction. I mentioned that I was aware of myself playing a role in our exchanges—the role of the "man of passion," the "irrepressible lover." It seemed important to do this, both for Cindy and myself—especially since her natural inclination was towards restraint and reality, rather than romance. It was as if I were continually trying to overcome her English reserve, and continually being checked and gently rebuffed. Which, despite all my protestations, I secretly wanted to be. If I wasn't rebuffed, what then? Our virtual adultery would become actual adultery, and I knew I couldn't handle that. Cindy knew it too. She probably couldn't have, either.

I felt guilty about what I was doing, of course. There was an undercurrent of guilt at all times during our correspondence. But it was never strong enough to make me stop, until that final year—and even then, there were a few lapses. The gratification of messaging was not only so instant, but also so easily available, since Cindy was online every weekday, when either Diane or I was usually at work (though, as I mentioned before, Diane's being home when I was didn't stop me either), that pleasure and excitement overrode guilt almost every time. (I even messaged with Cindy when Diane was in the hospital for reconstructive surgery, after the mastectomy, and then again for a serious infection, after that surgery failed.) My self-appointed role as the "man of passion" allowed me to deflect my guilt onto this person, who did not feel it as acutely as did the "husband of Diane" and the "father of Zack." For the "man of passion" had "natural urges" that were not to be denied. They beckoned continually to Cindy, without issue in the real world. But they must have given her some pleasure in our virtual world, because she did not tell me to stop. If she had, I would have. I mean, I think I would have—if only for reasons of pride (or vanity); for the idea of appearing to Cindy as a creep or a stalker was repulsive to me. (And also inconsistent with the role of the "man of passion.")

And how about the idea that I was hurting Diane every time I sent a message to Cindy—which was just about every weekday? It was more than just an idea. A betrayal is a fact, even if the one betrayed is not aware of it. And I never believed, even before she found out, that what Diane didn't know wouldn't hurt her, or wasn't hurting her. Furthermore, I knew that Diane was so acutely intuitive, and that we were connected so closely on an emotional and psychic level, that she must sense what was going on, and sooner rather than later.

Which she did. It came about through the heating up of our sex life. This had been very passionate in the early years. I remember how we would sometimes wake up in the middle of the night, as if on signal, and turn to each other, and come together, mouth to mouth, breast to breast, silently at first, and then not so silently. When she started to come, I made her moan into my mouth, for the downstairs neighbors' sake. I loved it. I drank up her moans like wine. But sometimes the moans would escape, like birds into the night. I loved that, too. But the comfort and ease we had always felt with one another ("It was like finally coming home"), and which was also a large part of our almost effortless sexual connection, could also lead to sexual indolence on my part. (She hardly ever refused an overture. I did. So much for the "man of passion.") Reading in bed became an end in itself, rather than a prelude or an aftermath.

And then there was the mastectomy. Physical mutilation is not a turn-on (at least not for me). Not to mention the shame, humiliation, and fear of rejection that Diane felt. The botched attempt at a breast implantation (the implant caused a serious infection and had to be removed) resulted in a nasty scar. The plastic surgeon responsible was a clean-cut, handsome, slick type whom I hadn't liked even before the surgery. After it, my dislike turned to repulsion, mixed with self-reproach. We should have gotten the best that New York City could offer to do the job. Why hadn't we? Didn't Diane deserve the best? And hadn't I been as lax as she in settling for this Long Island lothario? Here was the gruesome evidence of our laxity, which I tried to mitigate by a sick joke: It was as if someone had taken a machete to a painting by Rubens.

Beckett said "Habit is the great deadener," but it is also, for better or worse, the great softener. In time, I learned to focus my affections on the remaining breast, and even to see (or feel, because I usually avoided looking at it) the ribbed flatness on her left side as a novelty that was not without its own strange attraction.

As soon as the affair with Cindy started, however, the love-making with Diane suddenly became much more intense. It wasn't that I was fantasizing directly about Cindy when I was with Diane; it was rather that the awareness of the affair, and of my secret (and self-appointed) identity as "the man of passion," and of the secret life I imagined was connected with that iden-tity—the awareness of all of this flickered about our lovemaking, licking around the edges, spicing it up. The fantasy of my daily connection with another woman, whose real lover I had once been, and whose virtual lover I now was, began to burn into the reality of my nights with Diane. It didn't take her very long to notice the difference.

"Who is it, Josh?" she asked with a half-smile one evening. We were at a Japanese restaurant. The half-smile was because she was familiar—all too familiar—with my fantasies and little crushes over the years, most of which I shared with her, and none of which had come to anything (which was why I thought it was OK not to tell her about all of them). She always said, "As long as I benefit, I don't mind." There was no doubt she'd been benefiting recently, and she wanted to know to whom she could credit the pleasure. Of course there was a little hurt in that smile, too—but nothing that, in times past, I wouldn't have been able to soften by an assurance that this fantasy, like all the others, had and would come to nothing. That it was just a figment of my overactive imagination, with no past and no future. The current object of my fantasies would be named—if I even knew her name. (There was one woman at Warner Brothers with beautiful long red hair, and a slightly dumpy but for some reason provocative figure, whose name I didn't know, because I had never spoken or even come close to her, and whom I dubbed "Vespasia," for no reason at all, other than that naming her would disarm the fantasy. The absurder the name, the more disarming. Another woman at Warner Brothers was actually named "Capri." It only took Diane uttering the name a couple of times to do away with her.)

But this name was different. I knew that, which was why I didn't want to say it.

"Come on, Josh—spit it out. Who is it?"

I began to squirm and grimace like a child. The grimace was something I'd picked up from my late uncle—another sign of childish embarrassment that had become a joke between us. Sometimes Diane could feel me grimacing when we were hugging in the kitchen. The use of the grimace now was a vain attempt to dodge the seriousness of what I was about to tell her, to butter her up so that she wouldn't take it as hard as I knew she would.

But she wasn't in the mood for games. "Tell me."

As soon as I said the name—the name so fraught for both of us, not fictional or absurd this time, but beautiful, like the woman it belonged to—as soon as I said her name, "Cindy," with a sick, stupid sort of grin on my face, Diane's half-smile disappeared. But the grin remained stuck on my face, like a donkey's tail, or a dunce's cap.

"What's going on, Josh?" Her intent, level gaze met my confused one. "What are you doing?"

So I told her. Everything. What hurt her most was not the virtual flirtation, but the actual lunches.

"Nothing happened," I tried to reassure her—and myself.

"But you wanted it to," she replied. "And it would have. You betrayed me," she said matter-of-factly, with that same clear forthrightness she brought to all her dealings. That forthrightness of which I was, apparently, not capable. Not because I was a child, this time, but because I was unfaithful. I had betrayed her, just as she said.

From that moment in the Japanese restaurant, things were never quite the same between us. The knowledge of what I had done to her, to her trust—and therefore of what I was capable of, the capacity for hurt and treachery that I had within me—became something heavy that belonged to both of us, like an unditchable old suitcase. But, like that old suitcase (and I am thinking now of Diane's hard old blue-and-maroon, canvas-and-leather-covered suitcase, that she first took to Perry Mansfield Dance Academy in Steamboat Springs, Colorado, as a teenager, with her maiden initials, "D.A.," under the handle, and which Zack now uses, and will take to college), our knowledge of my betrayal was also a marker of trips and changes, endings and beginnings in our lives. Of new places reached, old places left behind. Sudden arrivals, and gradual, accustomed adaptations that could never have been foreseen in the strange newness of first days, which are later looked back upon from the vantage point of familiarity, as on a foreign land of olden times. And of our surprising ability to carry such a load of experiences—for better and worse, more than we ever thought we could—and survive. And sometimes, even, despite the accruing weight of years, to flourish.

Which our marriage did again too, eventually, in the last year of her life, when the cancer had metastasized into her abdomen and her illness became inoperable, and barely even treatable (almost constant pain and abdominal swelling). And when I finally stopped being angry at her for being sick, and feeling sorry for myself for being married to her. And when, also, I was finally able, during the last six months of that last year, to stop writing to Cindy. Our last year together is another story: a story of success, not of failure—unless it is the failure of life itself, 30 years too soon.

There is a coda to this story, though, that must be told—the worst part, by far. It is an aspect of my betrayal that Diane never knew about, and shows a side of my character that is less like an old suitcase than a poisonous snake.

At the first Christmas of the affair, before Diane had confronted me, and perhaps before she even knew (though I believe that deep down she always knew; and that I knew that she knew; and furthermore that it was important for me to know this: on some level it eased my conscience to believe that I wasn't getting away with anything)—on that first Christmas I sent Cindy a book of Blake's illuminated works, with a short inscription I had spent days composing in my head. The inscription read: "To Cindy: Somewhere, Somehow, Sometime."

What is truly horrible about what I wrote is not so much the deception involved, but the wish—and the hope, even—implied by that "somewhere, somehow, sometime." It was a wish, and a hope, that I wanted to convey to Cindy, without actually coming out and saying it: that after Diane had died, we would get together again. This idea was vaguely yet insistently present in my mind when I wrote the inscription: that there would be a life for me after Diane's death, and that I was imagining, and even hoping, that that life—or a part of that life, anyway—would be spent with Cindy. I wish I could say that I was drunk, or in the grip of an uncontrollable mania, when I wrote it. But while it is true that I am moderately manic-depressive ("cyclothymic" is the technical term), it was never the case that I didn't know what I was doing, or was unable to refrain from doing it. Impulsive, yes; uncontrollable, no. Even the addictive elements of our correspondence were, in a sense, willingly given into for the sake of being a "man of passion." I knew what I was writing; I knew the effect I wanted it to have; and I meant what I wrote, at least at the time that I wrote it. I was hedging my bets, and sugar-coating the wager with the language of love. It might even appear—it might even be the case—that I was betting against Diane. I was betting she would die. And I was right.

My monstrousness—I don't know what else to call it, and I don't believe this is too strong a word for what I did (no doubt others are capable of such a thing as well, but I don't think that most would allow themselves to actually write it, let alone inscribe it in a gift)—my monstrousness was not acted upon. I have not kept my implied promise to Cindy. Nor do I think, now, that I ever could. But any credit for my restraint—or rather, by now, my lack of desire (La Rochefoucauld: "When we resist our passions it is more on account of their weakness than our strength")—must go more to Diane than to me. (Even after death she is protecting me from myself.) A short while before she died, in one of her characteristically forthright moments, we were discussing—or rather, she was talking about it, because I could not discuss it, and evaded it at every opportunity—what would happen to me and Zack after she was gone. "I know you'll remarry," she said, "and I want you to. You won't be happy alone, and I want you to be happy. Just promise me you won't go with Cindy."

I promised. And I have kept that promise, at least. A promise that should never have had to be made in the first place.

One of my father's favorite maxims runs as follows: "Judge a writer by the best thing he's ever done, and a man by the worst."

In my case, another Hobson's choice.

12

My Failure as a Son

"The forces of life are seen in disguise,
A thousand disguises.
They make all things possible,
They guarantee nothing."

Euripides, *Bacchae*

In a phone conversation I had with my father sometime during the last few months of his life, when he was sounding particularly down, I asked him what was wrong. A stupid question, since at that point he was bedridden, incontinent, exhausted, and sometimes disoriented due to congestive heart failure. His answer was unexpected.

"You've disappointed me," he said.

"What do you mean, Gog?"

"I don't know. That's just how I feel."

"Boy, that's some feeling. Can you be a little more specific?"

"No," he said, irritated. "Just a feeling of general disappointment."

"With me?"

"Yes."

"Something I did to you? Or that I failed to do?"

"I don't want to talk about it," he snapped. "Let's just drop it."

So we did. He never mentioned it again, and neither did I. Now I wish I had. Even though there was no guarantee he would have told me anything, I should have tried anyway. Maybe it would have turned out that he'd forgotten all about it; or maybe he really hadn't been disappointed at all. Magical hopes, perhaps, but they were worth a try. And even if worse came to worst, and it turned out that I had done something serious to disappoint him, or had seriously neglected to do something, and he'd told me what it was, we might have talked about it. (This too was probably a magical hope, since he, a World War II veteran, wasn't of the generation to "talk about things.") We might have made things right between us. I could have asked his forgiveness for whatever it was before he died.

But it didn't happen that way. It happened quite differently.

I was with him when he died, late on a Sunday night, in Santa Monica Hospital, having gotten in from New York at 2 a.m. Saturday morning. I went right to the hospital, where his second wife, whom he'd married in 1998, and whom I'll call Jo-lin, had not left his side since he'd been admitted the previous day. Jo-lin, a clinically trained Chinese acupuncturist and herbologist, had been keeping him alive for over a year, ever since he'd suddenly collapsed in the dining room. (He remembered nothing of this. I wasn't there, but heard about it from Jo-lin, as well as from a former screenwriting student of my father's who'd been visiting at the time.) He had gone into cardiac arrest, stopped breathing, his face turned blue. The paramedics were there within minutes, but before they could apply the defibrillation paddles, which I guess she didn't like the looks of, Jo-lin cried "Wait!" She took an acupuncture needle, stuck it into his upper lip, right below his nose, and gave it a few twirls. His heart started beating again, he began to breathe, his eyes fluttered open, and he said, "What happened?"

When I told him, shortly after this, that Diane and Zack and I would be coming out to L.A. for a visit, not in time for Passover, but just in time for Easter, he shot right back, "Good—we can celebrate my resurrection."

The following October he had another crisis. This time I took a week off from classes and flew out to be with him. He'd been suffering for weeks from uncontrollable hiccups. The acupuncture and acupressure treatments Jo-lin was giving him worked only intermittently; but the tranquilizer the doctor had prescribed to stop the hiccuping cycle proved disastrous, relaxing his autonomic nervous system to the point where he was having trouble breathing. Jo-lin stopped giving him the tranquilizers, but then the hiccups came back. In desperation, while Jo-lin was out, I gave him a tranquilizer—even though she had told me not to—and the respiratory problems started again, now worse than ever. His breathing was shallow; his pulse was very weak. Jo-lin thought he might be dying. We spent an agonizing weekend that turned into a deathwatch, with my father lying inert in bed, needles sticking out of his head and arms. Then, on Monday, he turned a corner. He was breathing more easily; he sat up in bed; he asked for something to drink. If we'd had any doubts before, we now knew that Jo-lin was a miracle worker.

For the next six months there were no more crises. My father remained bedridden and very weak, but his vital signs were stable. When we flew out for Christmas and Easter, I cooked holiday meals and he ate well—even greedily, despite Jo-lin's admonitions. (My mother's had never had any effect on him either, and he ended up outliving her by nine years.)

Even a month later, in early May, 2004, after vomiting blood and being rushed back to Santa Monica Hospital, he seemed to be regaining his appetite. (Though his former characteristic vigor—Diane liked to point out that his initials, after all, were N.R.G., "energy"—was gone forever.) He scarfed down a plate of eggs for breakfast on Sunday. Was it my presence that had given him back his appetite? It was nice to think so. In any case, he certainly didn't seem "disappointed" then to see me. Even if I'd thought to ask him, which I didn't, it wouldn't have been the right time for us to talk about how I might have failed him, or his hopes for me, or whatever it was that had prompted that earlier remark.

Back at the house I'd found an old photo of the two of us, taken during a camping trip we'd made through Utah, Wyoming, Montana, and Idaho, the summer after my first year at Exeter. In the photo, we are sitting in Adirondack chairs on the sunny porch of our family doctor's cabin on Lake McDonald in Glacier National Park, Montana. My father is smoking his pipe; I am wearing a tall Stetson hat, and sitting next to him. Golden days of yore. The September after that photo was taken, my father had his first heart attack, which at the time he'd thought was a bad case of indigestion following a binge of Mexican food and ping-pong at his friend Mark Robson's birthday party. He spent a week in bed chugging Maalox (it was highly unusual for him to spend any waking hours in bed, no matter how bad he felt), until my mom made him go see Doc Beck, who ran an EKG and put him right in the hospital. But that September story only made the summer memory caught in this photo all the more golden. We would get steaks and cook them on disposable tinfoil grills. We would buy melons at farm stands and cool them in icy mountain streams, then eat them for dessert, after the steaks. That camping trip was the closest we'd ever been.

I handed him the photo now and said, "Remember this?"

"Yes," he said, with a little smile. (His "little smiles" at personal matters were always slightly shy and embarrassed.) "Doc Beck's cabin on the lake."

Even if I'd wanted to, even if I'd remembered, how could I have gone from that moment—that second moment, in the hospital, in remembrance of the first, on Lake McDonald—to the "disappointment" question? One would have to have the emotional equivalent of a tin ear to do that. Not to mention the likelihood of his snarled response: "What are you bringing up that crap for?" And he would have been right. In the remembered summer afternoon light of that porch on the lake, such psychological probings could only seem paltry and irrelevant.

In good time, I was to have an answer to my question—though not in a way I would ever have expected.

ॐ

Nearly two years later—on April Fool's Day, as it happened—I was sitting in the open-air rooftop bar of the Gansvoort Hotel in Greenwich Village, across from someone I'll call Jack Berg. Jack had been one of my father's best friends, and he had something he needed to get off his chest. I knew this, because he'd told me the previous December, and I'd been waiting for—and dreading—this meeting for months. It wasn't something we could talk about over the phone, he said. It had to be "man-to-man, eye-to-eye."

"Toe-to-toe also, Jack?" I'd joked, when he first mentioned it.

"I certainly hope not," he laughed. "But I don't think so."

"You don't *think* so? Geez, Jack, it must be pretty serious."

"Let's just say it's a discussion we need to have."

"But not over the phone?"

"Absolutely not."

"Boy. Well, I can't wait, Jack." He didn't laugh this time. "Maybe I should fly out there. If you think I should, I will. Tomorrow." (I was on sabbatical, so I could do that.)

"No, there's no need for that. The Academy owes me a trip, and I'm planning to come out there in March or April. It can wait til then." Jack had a production company that made trailers and teasers for movies, and some years back he'd directed a short that had been nominated for an Oscar, which had gotten him into the Academy of Motion Picture Arts and Sciences. He was also involved in the production of the Oscars show every year, and was on the governing board of the Academy. Definitely a player, as the saying goes. But a good man, and he'd been devoted to my father.

The rooftop bar was hopping, full of beautiful young people, and the view was spectacular—south and west out over the Hudson, to where the late-afternoon sun was sending godly-looking rays down through the clouds over Jersey. I was no longer dreading so much whatever it was Jack was about to tell me. We seemed to have re-established our friendly footing, even though what had originally prompted our meeting was Jack's comment, to a mutual friend, that "Josh and I aren't so friendly anymore." The comment had gotten back to me, and I had phoned Jack immediately—hence our earlier conversation, and now this meeting.

In the intervening few months I'd had lots of time to think about what it could be that he wanted to talk to me about—what had made him feel "not so friendly" towards me. I figured it must have something to do with my father, and I had finally settled on what I thought it was. Jack had not spoken at my father's memorial, and I remember at the time, and afterward, thinking this strange. But now I believed I knew the reason: It must be because I hadn't personally asked him to speak. I had called on a few other speakers by name, but not Jack. True, unlike the others, he hadn't given any indication that he wanted to speak, but I should have known anyway. I should have included him. After all, our family had known him since 1970, when I was 15, and Jack was in college, doing an internship as a production assistant on *The Andromeda Strain*, which my dad had written the screenplay for, and Bob Wise had directed. We even had the same birthday, Jack and I, and had celebrated a number of them together at the house in Pacific Palisades. To call us "old friends" would not get it exactly right: We were both less and more than that. Jack was really my parents' friend, not mine. Our relationship was almost one of siblings, birthday twins of a sort, born on the same day a few years apart. This quasi-fraternal relationship was enforced, in my mind at least, by the sense that my father's relationship with Jack went beyond friendship and had some of the qualities of a father–son connection. Jack's love for my father was almost filial.

From his easy, natural manner now, it was hard to take seriously his earlier comment to our mutual friend. We exchanged jokes and small talk, as we always did when we got together. We'd known each other so long that it wasn't hard to feel comfortable around each other, despite the apparently weighty nature of what we had to discuss. I felt confident that it would turn out to be much less serious than Jack had led me to expect by his insistence on a "man-to-man" meeting. In my experience—the experience of a habitual worrier—the actual future has almost always proved to be less unpleasant than the dread of it. I had worried so much about this meeting when Jack first expressed the need for it that, by now, my anxiety had pretty much burned itself out, and had provided a sort of overcompensating "insurance" that the reality would not be as upsetting as the fear of it.

"So," Jack began, "let's cut right to the chase. The day that Nelson died, or maybe it was the day before, he was apparently given some medication that Jo-lin felt may have shortened his life. She wasn't there at the hospital when they gave him the medication, but apparently you were. She said she had left instructions with you that they weren't to give him medication of any sort, because he was having trouble breathing. Like that time the previous October, when he was having trouble breathing because of the medication you gave him for the hiccups he was having. You remember that?"

"Yes, I do." I wasn't quite seeing where this was going.

"And he was having hiccups just before he died, too, wasn't he? I seem to remember that."

"Yes, he was. We were giving him acupressure for that. I remember Jo-lin showing me the pressure point on the inside of his wrist where I had to press."

"Right. But apparently they also, at some point, when she wasn't there, but you were, gave him medication—the same medication that almost killed him when you gave it to him back in October. And Jo-lin felt at the time—this is right after he died—that if he hadn't gotten that medication in the hospital, he might have had a few more days. He might have been able to come home. Because they were getting ready to release him the following day, weren't they?"

"Yes, I remember that."

"But instead, he died." Jack was speaking very carefully, very deliberately, and watching me intently. In a friendly way, but intently.

"Jack, what are you saying?"

He paused and drew back a bit. "I'm saying there is a possibility—just a possibility, that's all it is, and we'll never know for sure, so it's really all just conjecture—but a possibility, at least Jo-lin seemed to feel so at the time, that if they hadn't given him that medication in the hospital, he might have lived a few more days. *Might have*. And gotten to go home, as he wanted to do. As we all wanted him to do. But instead, he died in the hospital. But as I say," he was quick to add, "there is no way we'll ever know for sure, so it all remains highly speculative."

"So what are you saying, Jack? Are you saying I let them kill my father?"

Heads turned, but I kept my eyes on Jack, whose expression hadn't changed: direct, intent, not unfriendly. My question had sounded so unreal, so melodramatic, that I couldn't help smiling as I phrased it. Yet Jack was not smiling.

"I wouldn't put it that way," he said. Not "Of course not!" or "Don't be ridiculous!" but "I wouldn't put it that way."

My ears were beginning to ring now, and a mist—what later that night, on the long walk from the hotel to Penn Station, and then from Huntington Station home, I was to think of as the Buddhists' "great cloud of unknowing"—seemed to come over my mind. The cityscape around us began to tilt, as if the Earth's axis had shifted a little. And for me, I suppose it had.

"You wouldn't put it that way," I repeated. "Well then, how

would you put it?" My voice sounded disembodied—as disembodied as the weird smile on my face. The smile of disbelief. Or of unknowing. Or of just not understanding. The great smile of just not understanding.

Jack sat back again, choosing his words carefully. "I would say, I just don't know." Again, not "Of course you didn't let them kill your father!" but simply, "I just don't know."

"What do you mean, Jack?"

"I mean it is useless to speculate, because there is no way we will ever know any of these things. Which is why I didn't want to even mention it to you in the first place. But when you called, I realized I had to."

"Mention *what*, Jack? We will never know *what things*, Jack? What the hell are you talking about? Are you saying what I think you're saying? That I let them kill my father? Do you even know what you are saying?"

"Yes, I do. I do know what I'm saying, Josh. Which is why I'm being very careful, and I'm not saying that. All I'm saying, again, is that according to Jo-lin, the medication was given to him on your watch, after she expressly told you—again, according to her—and I'm just going by what she told me, and then there is the whole language thing with her, too. But according to what I understood from her, she left instructions with you before she left the hospital not to let them give him any medications at all, out of a fear of a replay of last October, when that medication—which you gave him, again against her instructions—almost killed him."

I opened my mouth, but nothing came out. I shook my head, as though to clear it, but the mist remained, and the cloud grew larger.

"I can't believe this is happening," I said. "I can't believe we are having this conversation, Jack."

He gave a wry laugh. "Believe me, Josh, it's not my idea of a good time, either. I never wanted to have to tell you this."

"Would you have? If Jess [our mutual friend] hadn't called

me, would you have told me? Or would you just have kept this thing inside and never have told me?"

He looked at me. "I don't know."

"You don't know? Like you don't know whether I killed my father or not?"

"I never said that, Josh."

"In so many words, Jack, you did. You said I let them give him medication that killed him—or might have killed him. And before that, when he was having the hiccuping attack back in October, you said I went against Jo-lin's orders and gave him medication that almost killed him. That would have killed him, if she hadn't saved his life. 'Again.' Like I'm trying to kill him, and thank God she's there to save his life. That's what I'm hearing, Jack."

"Well if that's what you're hearing, then I must not be communicating my message very well. Probably not. Because, most assuredly, that is not what I'm saying." He paused. "As I told you, I never wanted to have this discussion, but when you called last Christmas, I realized it was inevitable."

"Is that supposed to make me feel better? That you never wanted to tell me your suspicions, but finally had to?"

"No, that's not it at all. What I meant was, I don't know if those suspicions, as you call them—I would call them questions—have any basis whatsoever in fact. As far as I know, they don't."

"*As far as you know*. Wow. You mean, there is a possibility that they *do*. There is a possibility—even the remotest of possibilities—that I wanted, or allowed, my father to die."

"Stop saying that. That's not what I'm saying."

Now I could feel the beautiful people around us making a deliberate effort not to look at us, while at the same time wanting to overhear every word of this very strange conversation. More than they'd bargained for in this scenic, romantic spot, on this mild spring evening. Certainly more than I'd bargained for. Not in my wildest dreams....

"I know you loved your father," Jack began carefully. "And that you hated to see him suffering. We all did. Jo-lin was doing all in her power, as you well know, to keep him from suffering, and also to keep him alive. And she was doing a great job in both of those regards." He paused. "And I guess there was just some question of whether you and she were on the same page in that regard."

"Meaning?"

"Meaning what I just said. That maybe you and she weren't on the same page. That's all I mean, Josh. There's nothing more to it than that."

But it sounded to me, from his careful circumlocutions, like there was a lot more to it than that—and that "that," whatever it was, was much worse than it sounded, worse than he wanted to say.

"But Jack, you make it sound like I didn't agree that she should do everything she could to keep him alive. Is that what you think? Is that what she thinks?"

He looked at the table and shook his head. "Absolutely not. No one is saying that. Or thinking that. Certainly not me. And while I don't presume to speak for Jo-lin, I would be very surprised if she thought that." He brought his eyes back to mine, and gazed at me levelly.

"So what *do* you think? Why are we even having this conversation? What is going on?"

"Believe me," he said, with another wry laugh, "this is almost as hard for me as it is for you."

"I doubt that. You're not the one being accused of killing your father."

"Come on, Josh."

"Or whatever it is I'm being accused of. Because I definitely feel I'm being accused of something. I'm just not sure what it is."

"I'm sorry you feel that way. Really. An accusation was the farthest thing from my mind in having this conversation. I understand your reaction, but it's definitely not an accusation. Nothing of the sort."

"Then what the fuck sort of thing is it, Jack? Would you please tell me what is going on?"

The rooftop bar and all the people and the cityscape around us and the whole spring evening had suddenly turned spooky—distant, alienated, as if they contained some message I couldn't quite decipher. It was an atmosphere I recognized from Diane's last days, and the days and weeks after her death. The spookiness of death, of irretrievable loss. The spookiness of being suddenly alone, of a loneliness so profound it cannot even be recognized as such, but only as…spookiness. Perhaps that is what ghosts are: just a way for us to name, and therefore understand, the profound and irremediable loneliness that follows a death. And add to that, now, the utter weirdness of being thought to have caused, in some way or another, my father's death; and also of not knowing whether or not there might even be some truth in this. Jack had said, "I don't know." He was being honest. Maybe I didn't know, either. Maybe my motives were beyond me.

"There is no question that you loved your father," he began again. "It must have torn you up inside to see him suffering. It tore me up, and I can only imagine—no, I can't even imagine—what you must have been going through." Once again he met my eyes with his direct, level, not-unfriendly gaze. Birthday twins, remember? "Which would explain your attitude to the medication, and your differences with Jo-lin in that regard."

He kept his eyes on mine, and finally it sank in, with a little plop.

"You mean I wanted to put my dad out of his suffering."

"Not necessarily. Not actively."

"But passively. Whatever that means. You tell me, Jack. You seem to know what was in my mind better than I do."

"I don't know anything, Josh. No one does, and no one ever will."

"But you seem to know enough to accuse me—sorry, to

suggest that I might have wanted to put my father out of his suffering, if not actively, then passively. Either kill him, or let him die. With the best of intentions, of course. Isn't that what you're insinuating?"

"You're being unfair."

"Unfair? Am I? Who's being unfair, Jack? Don't you think it's a little bit unfair to accuse—to suggest that there is even the slightest possibility that I would want to do anything, anything, to hurt my father? I think that's being a little unfair, don't you? We may not have had the greatest relationship in recent years, but *he was my father*, Jack. He wasn't your father, he was mine."

Jack nodded calmly, folding his arms on the table. "All the more reason why you wouldn't want to see him suffer."

"And would want him to die instead?"

Jack sat back again. "I'm just telling you what's—what I've been carrying around for almost two years, Josh. I'm not saying there's necessarily any truth to it. But we've known each other a long time, and I had to get it off my chest."

"And onto mine."

"That wasn't my intention, but that's how it worked out. If I'd had my druthers, Jess wouldn't have called you in the first place."

"But you still would have thought what you thought—and still think, apparently—and I'd never have known."

"Well, I'm not sure what purpose is served by having you know. It won't change anything."

"But it's the truth, Jack. It's what you really think. We've known each how long? Over 35 years. Do you really think I would be capable of such a thing?"

"I would like to think not, Josh, but—"

"You would 'like to think not'? Gee thanks, Jack."

"What I mean is, our motives are complicated. All of our motives are complicated, irregardless of what we might like to think. There aren't many people out there who act from absolutely pure motives. I know I don't. And I imagine you don't, either. And while we might like to think they are pure, they usually aren't. And sometimes it's a real jumble, especially at times of extreme stress and uncertainty, like it was with your father at the end of his life. The right decision is very hard to make at such times. And maybe there is no right decision."

"But you think I made the wrong decision."

He sighed. "We seem to be going in circles."

"I'll say."

"Let me try once more to put it exactly as I see it. Taking into account your unquestionable love for your father, and also the 'fog of war' of the situation at the time—which is a term I'm sure he would have found appropriate. Ironically so."

"Go ahead, Jack. I'm all ears."

He took a sip of beer; meanwhile, I had been knocking back cup after cup of tea from the large pitcher the waitress had brought.

"As I said before, you and Jo-lin just weren't on the same page. She wanted to keep him alive as long as possible—as comfortable as possible, but also as long as possible. That was her primary obligation as she saw it, as his primary caregiver. Your obligation—or call it your wish, your concern, was different. You didn't want to see him suffer. You wanted him to be comfortable too, of course—not to suffer from the hiccups, not to be disoriented—though the medication, as I understand it, made him even more disoriented—and not to be cursing out the nurses, which I remember your saying he was doing."

"So I killed him," I said. This time it was me giving him the level gaze, poker-faced and unflinching. We stared at each other for a few seconds, and then he broke into a laugh.

"Right, Josh—you killed him. That's just what I think. You nailed it, man." He took another sip of his beer.

"But really, that's not too far from what you're saying, Jack. What does it matter whether it was active or passive, negligence or euthanasia—it all amounts to the same thing, doesn't it? My father was given possibly fatal medication on my watch, and so

I'm responsible. Or partly responsible. I'm at least partly responsible for his death. Isn't that what you're saying?"

Jack shook his head and smiled. "We seem to be going in circles again. I foresaw that this might happen, which was one of the reasons I didn't want to have this discussion. It doesn't seem to have accomplished anything except getting you upset, for no reason."

"I wouldn't call having one of your oldest friends think you may be responsible for your father's death 'no reason,' would you, Jack? I would say it's a pretty good reason to get upset. It's the best reason to get upset that I've had all day. But I want to go back to this euthanasia thing," I said.

"I never mentioned the word 'euthanasia'."

"I know you didn't. But that's essentially what it is, Jack—that I may have knowingly let them give him medication that was fatal because I wanted him to die sooner rather than later."

"There's a big difference between that and euthanasia, Josh."

"Call it what you want. But if you're saying that I did anything, even passively, for whatever reason, even a good one, to help shorten my father's life by even a day or two, I don't really see the difference. It's a big fucking thing, whatever you want to call it. Otherwise we wouldn't even be having this discussion. Obviously, you thought it was important enough that you had to say something. I just wish you'd said something sooner, rather than keeping it inside."

"I already told you, Josh—I just didn't see what it would accomplish. And I still don't. What's done is done."

"But that's just it, Jack. What *was* done? That's the whole point, isn't it? Not that he died, but how he died. You're saying he died before he had to, because of something I did or didn't do, and I just can't let that go unchallenged."

Who was I trying to convince—him or me? I didn't even know anymore; besides, it didn't matter. Now that his doubts had been aired, I knew they would never go away, as far as I was concerned. And yet I kept talking. What else could I do? Accept a tacit condemnation in silence?

"You don't need to challenge anything, Josh. I told you, there's no accusation here. Not even close."

"Well, I appreciate your saying that, but whatever you want to call it, there has obviously, in your eyes, been a wrong committed, for which I am in some way responsible. But my father never, at any point, said anything about euthanasia, or wanting to end his life, or whatever you want to call it. Besides, euthanasia just wasn't his style. He was a fighter—he was always a fighter. You know that as well as I, Jack."

"Yes, he was."

"And he was fighting up to the very end. I was with him. I was holding his right hand, and Jo-lin was holding his left hand, and he was struggling for breath, and I was saying to him, 'Keep fighting, Gog, keep fighting. Don't give up. Keep on fighting.' And that's how he died, Jack. That's how he wanted to die, and that's how he died. And that seemed absolutely right."

The sun was setting now over Jersey, and the air was getting chilly. I was wearing a jacket, but Jack wasn't. He buttoned up his shirt and crossed his arms again on the table. He had finished his beer, and I had finished my tea. He paid the bill, and we both stood up.

"But I have a feeling that nothing I have said, or can say, will remove the doubt from your mind," I told him. "Is that true?"

"I certainly hope not, Josh. I certainly hope it isn't true."

"But you're not sure."

"No," he said, "I'm not sure. But that may change as a result of our meeting and talking about these things. I hope it does change."

I sighed. "Well Jack, at this point, then, there appears to be only one thing left for me to do." I stood up on my chair and made as if to jump over the parapet to the pavement below. He laughed his open-mouthed laugh, while turning his shoulder a little to one side: a characteristic gesture of his, that reminded me of the way he had always laughed at my jokes. I felt the sweet acceptance of laughter. It wouldn't last long, but it helped us part as friends.

"April Fool's, right?" Jack laughed. "I only wish."

It wasn't until later, on the long walk uptown to Penn Station, that I wondered whether we would ever see each other again.

The next night, I phoned Jo-lin. I told her I had spoken to Jack, and the gist of what we had talked about: that I might have been partly responsible, in one way or another, for my father's death. I asked her if she had felt that way when he died, and if she felt that way now.

Her answers to my questions, like Jack's, were very careful. Unlike some people, I never had much trouble understanding Jo-lin's broken English—her meaning was always clear to me. But now, because of her carefulness, and my attentiveness, her words carried a particular weight, and there was much that could be heard between the lines.

"Josh, I feel you are a good son," she began, hesitantly. "But the medication they give Nelson in the hospital was not good."

"Do you think it shortened his life?"

"I do not understand 'shorten'."

"Was the—do you think the medicine they give him in hospital make him die?" The pidgin English I found myself falling into with her gave a particularly surreal aspect to the question—and to our whole conversation. But the basic, unadorned, even crude quality of our language made what we were saying all the more stark and unavoidable.

"It is hard to say," she replied. "Josh, that medicine not good for him. That medicine make him more sick."

"Do you think it was my fault that they gave him that medicine, Jo-lin?"

"Not your fault, no," she said quickly. "You are good son. You did not know." But besides the suspicious quickness of her response, there was also a reserve, a holding back in her voice that I did not find reassuring. I had to push it further.

"Jack Berg thinks I might have wanted Nelson to die sooner, so he wouldn't suffer. Do you think that too, Jo-lin?"

"I don't know, Josh. I don't know what is in your mind."

So there it was. The same thing Jack had said. Different words, different voice—but the same meaning. The same doubt. The same unthinkable question that both of them seemed to be unable not to think.

"I will tell you now what is in my mind, Jo-lin. And I swear this is the truth. I never wanted to do anything, *anything*, to hurt my father. Including anything to shorten his life, to make him die. I wanted him to live, Jo-lin. I wanted him to live as much as you wanted him to live."

I heard her take a breath, as if she were taking in everything I had just said, and trying to decide what to keep and what to discard.

"I believe you are good son, Josh," she repeated.

"But do you believe I did not want Nelson to die? Do you believe I wanted him to live?"

She waited a few beats before repeating, "It is hard to say."

Now I waited, unsure of what to say next—or even if I wanted to say anything. With Jack, the conversation had been propelled along by the sheer energy of incredulity, suspicion, and outrage. With Jo-lin, the conversation seemed to break on the naked rocks of truth. But how could it be true? How could I be me, and it be true?

"Jo-lin. It hurts me very much for you to think that."

The words sounded insipid and insincere as I spoke them, and they still do. Perhaps, though, this insipidity was one more aspect of the surreal disconnect between our conversation, the words of our conversation, and the reality of what was being thought, suspected, concealed, unspoken—the reality of what would never be known, but still could be imagined: the worst of what a person, in this case me, could be capable of doing.

"It hurts me very much for you to think that I would do anything, knowingly or unknowingly, to hurt my father, or take life from him. How can you think that, Jo-lin? Do you know what you are saying? Do you know what that means?"

A long, audible breath. "Yes, Josh, I know. I know what means. I will tell you. You not only one who hurt. I think you are good son, but sometimes you are very angry at your father. One time, upstairs, in study, you very, very angry. Nelson, he was very mean sometimes to Diane. He say terrible things to her. He very mean to me too, sometimes. He say terrible things, maybe he don't mean, I think he don't mean. But you very angry. And you tell to me, 'Jo-lin, next time he have heart attack, you don't save him, you let him die.'"

As before, with Jack, there was a ringing in my ears. It didn't go away. I had to speak through it. "Did I really say that, Jo-lin?"

"Yes, Josh, you say that. It hurt me very, very much. I love Nelson very much. I do not think you can say that about your father."

My mouth opened and closed a couple of times, but no words came out. I remember thinking that this must be what was referred to as being at a loss for words. When I finally found my voice, it was trembling.

"Jo-lin, sometimes, when we very angry, we say things we don't mean."

"Yes, I know. You do not mean." She didn't sound convinced.

"And I would never, ever, do anything to hurt him, however angry I might have been. I want you to believe that, Jo-lin. Do you believe that?"

"Josh, you good son," she repeated. It sounded almost automatic by now. Something kept pushing me forward.

"Jo-lin, did my father think that?"

"He think…?" After a moment of silence, I realized she was not waiting to formulate a response, but for me to repeat my question.

"Did my father think I was a good son? Did he ever say to you that I was a bad son?"

Another long pause before answering. "He never say to me that."

"Did he ever say anything *like* that?"

"What he like?"

"No, did he—let me tell you why I ask this question, Jo-lin. My father once say to me, he say, 'You have disappointed me.' Do you know what he mean by that?"

"I do not understand 'dispoint'."

"He say to me that I did not do what he want me to do. That I make him sad because I do not do what he want. Did he ever say that to you?"

"Josh, I tell you. Nelson once say to me, 'All Josh want is the house.'"

"He really said that?"

"Yes, he say that. Maybe he angry at you when he say that."

"I guess so."

"Maybe he angry because you always in guest room," she added.

"What?"

"When you come with Diane and Zack to see him, you always in guest room."

"That's not true, Jo-lin—I came out to see him. I mean, I came out to Los Angeles to see him."

"I know, but you spend most of time in guest room."

"That's simply not true, Jo-lin," I said, my voice trembling again, my heart down around my knees. What made it even worse was that there was no accusation in her voice—not even the careful, veiled, reluctant accusation that Jack had made (or rather tried, not quite successfully, not to make). Jo-lin's words were the simple voice of true observation. She had not been able not to notice.

Not to notice what? That while she was changing my father's diapers, I was off in another room. That when Jack Berg arrived after midnight to sit with him while he slept, or couldn't sleep, I myself was sound asleep—in the guest room. That when I did come into his room, I didn't spend very long in there, and usually brought a book along with me. Why? Because it was boring. Because we didn't have all that much to say to one another. Because even though, during the last year of his life, I only spent a few weeks with him, I did my best—unconsciously, perhaps; or perhaps not so unconsciously—to limit even that little time to the bare minimum.

Was this the whole truth about our relationship, that last year of his life? I remember that sometimes, when I came into his room with a book, I would bring a newspaper for him, or the book of photos of Old Havana I had bought for him. He had gone there several times after the war, after his novel was published (and maybe even before), when he was a young author, whose talents not only "would be heard from" but were being heard from, or were about to be heard from. He had gone to Hemingway's bar, "La Floridita," where, he told me, they squeezed whole pineapples in a special whole-pineapple-squeezer, then added enough rum to make you fall off your barstool. (Hem, of course, hadn't fallen off *his* barstool.) My father had met the Great Man himself, and had him sign a copy of *The Green Hills of Africa*. (I have this too, right next to my father's prison camp manuscript.) Hem signed it "With very [or "my"] best wishes, Ernest Hemingway, La Habana, 1936." Maybe the misdating was due to the rum drink; or maybe Hem was thinking of his glory days in the Spanish Civil War; or maybe it was a little bit—or a lot—of both, which is the version I prefer.

During the last year of his life, I would sit on the sofa in my father's bedroom, facing him, and he would soon fall asleep with the paper or the Old Havana book in his lap. It was nice being with him like that—both of us reading, or trying to read. Books and writing, after all, were what we had in common. Sports had only had a small place in our life together. We went to a few baseball and football games together, and in seventh grade, that miserable year, when I had needed his support so badly, and he had given it, we used to watch football games on Sunday. But neither of us was really a sports fan. Furthermore, he was always uncomfortable in a more traditional fatherly role. He would express that discomfort by giving me deliberately corny father-to-son Hallmark cards for Christmas and my birthday, and I did the same. We thus showed ourselves contemptuous of, and superior to, the imagined fathers and sons for whom the cornball cards were fabricated.

But underneath the ironic posturing—mine, anyway, but I suspect his too—there was an unironic son yearning to come out: yearning to call my father "Dad" instead of the bizarre, infantile-sounding "Gog"; yearning to play catch with him on a regular basis (instead of just a handful of times, which, because of their infrequency, I treasured all the more, yet whose very infrequency made me so self-conscious that I was unable to freely enjoy them while they were happening). Yearning to go to a football game with him and not have him wear his earring—presumably as a form of protest against the more conventional father role he saw himself in danger of falling into. I remember someone at a Rams' game throwing a hot dog at us and calling us "faggots." (This was in 1967, before earrings for men—not to mention fathers and sons—had caught on. My father's earring, however, went back to the late 1940s—Haiti this time, and a drunken evening in the bar of the Hotel Olaffson in Port au Prince, when his friend Maurice De Young, himself a kind of Hemingway figure, and part-owner of the hotel, had pierced his ear with an ice pick and then inserted a gold pirate's earring into the bloody hole.)

Yes, I yearned for a more traditional father, just as I also yearned for a more traditional mother—one who would bake cookies and listen to Frank Sinatra, instead of sometimes baking hash brownies and listening to the Stones.

But, as Jack Berg rightly said, this isn't about the blame game—or at least not about me blaming them. They were, both of them, free spirits, birds of youth, romantic lovers first and last, who made up the parenting thing as they went along. And somehow, they made it work. Not so different from Diane and me; and I know they loved me no less than we love Zack. (I use the first person plural, present tense, because I must believe that her love for him, as for me, is an uncanny and sensible power in the present, a force that has outlived her death. Certainly that is what it *feels* like, to me.) If there is any blame to be meted out, it is (surprise!) the blame I put on myself, for not being attentive enough, present enough, loving enough, to my father.

Perhaps it all boils down to this: not loving him enough. How much is "enough"? Maybe enough is not even having to ask the question.

There is much guilt around all of this, of course—going back to the day in 4th Grade when my mother told me that my father had said to her that when I left for school in the morning I never said goodbye to him, even though he always said goodbye to me. "Sometimes I feel like he doesn't even notice me," he'd said. I was stricken with guilt. For the next several months I made a deliberate—too deliberate—effort to notice my father, to be nice to him, to never forget to say goodbye and hello to him. To prove to him I loved him. (A sort of only child's King Lear syndrome.) This produced a noticeable and immediate change for the better in our relationship (though before my mother's remark to me I had not been aware there was anything wrong with our relationship). I remember being highly gratified by the thought that I could solve, and apparently so easily, with a minimum of effort, a problem that I hadn't even known was there—but that, once it had been pointed out, had mortified me. The reality, of course, was that the problem was not so easily solved. It required much deliberate effort on both our parts, and so the solution was a phony one—and the problem ultimately not solved at all. The painful truth was—is—that there was a fundamental disconnect between my father and me that we could never quite overcome, though from time to time we both tried. But never at the same time. Maybe that was part of the problem. Maybe even the biggest problem. After the conversation with Jo-lin, I saw that in her eyes—and therefore partly in mine, and maybe even in my father's—Jack Berg had been more of a son to him, and a better one, than I had. Maybe that's what he meant when he said that I had disappointed him.

Because my father saw himself as a "figure of pathos" (though he himself never used this term), I suppose it was only natural that I should learn to do the same—aided and abetted by my mother, the Queen of Pathos. Though it would be hard to say which aspects of his pathos I absorbed from his self-representations, and which from her projections. There surely must also have been some that came directly from my own perceptions of him—filtered, inevitably, through the other two, though arising from my own not inconsiderable endowments in the pathos department. I remember a few of these, dating from different periods of my life.

The first comes from a time when I could have been no more than six or seven. My father was sitting in a chair in the backyard, eating Frosted Flakes directly from the box. (At this time of his life he was overweight and diabetic—no surprise, given his snacking habits.) I told my mother that I felt sorry for him—the sort of thing that invariably brought tears to her eyes. Was that perhaps why I told her in the first place? Not that it gave me any pleasure to see her cry (much less *make* her cry); quite the opposite. But it did give me pleasure for her to praise me as a—what? "Child of pathos?" When two "figures of pathos" produce an offspring, what can he be but a "child of pathos"? If I were a Greek god—the god of failure, no doubt: *Pathetikos*, a minor deity (indeed, the god of minordom itself, and the tutelary spirit of losers, hacks, and Vegas comedians)—I probably would have sprung full-blown from the bleeding heart of my mother. In any case, her reaction to my perception of my father, stuffing his face with Frosted Flakes in the lawn chair, did much to ingrain that image in my memory.

The second image is from my mid-20s, and partly due to a hangover (the form that hangovers take with me being, often, uncontrollable weeping). It was the summer I had returned temporarily from New York and was living with my parents in Pacific Palisades, writing my novel. I got home late one night, after having had a few. My parents, who'd had dinner guests earlier in the evening, had gone to bed. On the coffee table in the living room was a thick book of my father's: Paul Scott's *The Raj Quartet*. A book I knew I would never read—nor, I suspected, would he, though he dug into it now and then. (It was a subject that interested him, and there was a personal aspect to his interest as well, since he'd written the screenplay for that movie about Gandhi's assassination.) I thought I could reconstruct the course of events that had brought the book onto the coffee table. At some time during the evening, they had gotten onto the subject of India, or Gandhi, or the British Empire, and my father, as he so often did, had gotten a book to show his friends, as part of his show-and-tell. It was always important to have a book as a kind of conversational prop. (And also as a kind of agent of validation for his own enthusiasms.) I could picture him so well, getting excited as he talked about the book, then going off into his study to fetch it; and the dinner guests politely examining the weighty tome, then setting it aside. When the guests left, my father went to bed, and the large, unread book remained on the coffee table. While registering all of this in my alcohol-softened brain, I did not even pause to pick up the book as I crossed the living room to my room. The next day I was hung over, and *The Raj Quartet* remained on the coffee table. At one point during that day of jumpy nerves I noticed it again, and something came over me. I went into my room, closed both doors, and fell onto my bed, weeping. I wept for about 15 minutes straight, my face buried in the pillow. A 24-year-old man convulsed by a fit of uncontrollable sobbing, caused by he knew not what: my father, his pathos, the book that no one would read (at least no one in this family), the imagined show-and-tell. But I do know this: the figure of my father as I had always known him (or was it as I had always imagined him?)—a figure innocent, guileless, childlike, vulnerable—was at the center of my weeping. This time, of course, I did not run to my mother and tell her I felt sorry for him; I kept it to myself. By that evening I felt better—and *The Raj Quartet*, thank God, had been put back in the library. (The summer after my father died, while I was packing up the house, I found it in his study. I could not bring myself to donate it, even though I still know I will never read it. It is important that I keep it always, so that I can think of him every time I see it and do not read it. However, on those days when I am hung over, I will avert my eyes from it, as though it were an Ark—the Sacred Ark of *Pathetikos*.)

The third image of my father has to do with the chest of hand puppets, and the small puppet theater, that he gave to Zack on his fifth birthday. Many of the puppets were reversible: a frog that turned inside out into a prince; a shoe that turned into Old Mother Hubbard; a rabbit, with a carrot in its mouth, that came out of a top hat. My father had loved puppets as a boy, and had had a puppet theater, where he and his brother put on shows. Now he was passing those pleasures on to his grandson. Except it didn't quite turn out that way. A friend and I put together an impromptu medley of fractured fairytales, but it was hard to keep the kids' attention, because we weren't exactly professionals, and we couldn't compete with the videos and video games they were already used to—nor with the life-size, remote-controlled robot I had hired for the party, built and operated by a retired engineering professor from Cal Tech. Thank God I wasn't hung over that day, or the puppet show might have turned into a child's version of *Death of a Salesman* (my father's oft-quoted favorite).

Why linger over these pathetic old chestnuts? Surely the sense of pathos, of a father's pathos, is no substitute for being a "good enough" son; for having "disappointed" him; for doing, at the end of his life, what I should have done for him—or at least (once again) for not doing what I shouldn't have done. What do I expect to accomplish by this pathetic coda? Do I hope, for instance, that Jack Berg will read it, that it might serve as the explanation, justification, vindication of my actions—or nonactions—that I failed to supply at the time of our rooftop meeting? An explanation that might go somewhat as follows:

"Hey Jack, listen. You may have been a better, more dutiful, more attentive, more concerned son to my father than I was—you who were not even related to him—but *I sure felt sorry for him.* Doesn't that count? I felt a lot sorrier for him than you ever did—maybe even than you ever could. Feeling sorry for people isn't your thing. You're a man of action, not sentiment. You're interested in results, and feeling sorry is a dead end. I know. And you're probably right. But I can't help it, I'm built that way. And was nurtured that way, too—bottle-fed on pathos, by two masters of the genre. And who knows—maybe feeling sorry for my father will help take some time off my stay in purgatory, where they send sons who did not love their fathers enough. But maybe that's just wishful thinking on my part. Maybe I'm not even headed for purgatory. OK, then—but maybe feeling sorry for him, since childhood, from the bottom of my slightly rotten heart, will at least get me a place in a higher circle of hell, where they send sons who are partly responsible, in some way or other, for their fathers' deaths.

"I know, Jack—you're a Jew, and don't believe in such things. So am I, sort of. Except I do sort of believe in them. At least to the extent that I believe that purgatory and hell—but not paradise—are right here on Earth. And let's not forget either that all that Catholic stuff (I'm writing this on Holy Tuesday, by the way; or, if you prefer, Passover Eve) goes back to a perversion of Judaism, anyway.

"Maybe what I'm trying to say to you, Jack—and Jo-lin too, while we're at it—is just this: That while the sense of pathos is not the same thing as love, you can't really have love without a sense of pathos. A sense of pathos softens the way for love, softens the core at the heart of love, so that the arrows of love can penetrate the 'soft core.' We can't love without loving also the vulnerability of the beloved. Someone who isn't vulnerable—or who doesn't at least seem vulnerable to us—isn't lovable, either. Love is a way of protecting the vulnerable, protecting 'the soft core' that enables love in the first place.

"I know, Jack—metaphysics, even a metaphysics of love, is no substitute for right action. No substitute for adequate love. For being the son I should have been. But let us also not forget—or let me also not forget, because you didn't see it, Jack, you weren't there; though perhaps if you had been, if you had seen it, it would have gone better between us—let me not forget the quote from George Eliot that I saw on the billboard on the railroad overpass in Worcester, MA: 'It is never too late to be what we might have been.' What a cheering thought! And maybe it's more than just a thought. Maybe it's the beginning of an action, a right action.

"The action of being a better son to you, Gog, even after you are gone (if that makes any sense). And maybe the start of this action is in writing—that action whose performance we shared, you and I. That action which is also a curious mélange of thinking and doing, a response and prelude to other thoughts and actions. Let the recognition of my failure as a son be not a sentence, either to hell or purgatory, but just the sign of a better beginning."

(Now I seem to hear a voice from the Other Side: growling, impatient, yet affectionate, in spite of itself):

That's good. Good ending. Though there's not much humor in any of this chapter. You should use more humor. I'm always telling you that. But the ending works pretty well. Still needs a rewrite, though. Cut out all the philosophy crap—just bogs it down. It's a mistake. But overall, the ending works pretty well.

"Thanks, Gog. I sort of like the philosophy, though. But maybe I can cut it in places."

Of course you can. Remember, most editing is just cutting.

"I know, you always said that."

Still do. Because it's true. (Suddenly frowning.) *Now I've got to get back to work. This is a real piece of crap I'm working on, you know.*

"But you'll make it better, right?"

No—less bad. I can only make it less bad. That's all I can do with this thing.

"Well, maybe that's good enough."

No, it isn't. Which is why I always tell you, if you're going to be a writer—

"Be a real writer ..."

Not a screenwriter. That's right.

"But, Gog?"

(Frowning again.) *What is it? I told you, I have to get back to work.*

"Just one thing. Did I fail you as a son?"

(Frowning even worse now, getting angry.) *Listen, I don't have time for that crap. I heard what Jack and Jo-lin said, and it's all a bunch of crap. I have to work.*

"I know. It's just that Jack and Jo-lin—"

(Really angry now, almost snarling.) *I told you, this whole damn thing is just bullshit. Just psychological bullshit. You spend too much time on that crap. Always did. Worrying about this, analyzing that, when what you should be doing is writing. They're not writers. They don't know what they're talking about.* (Pulling himself up in his swivel chair, half-facing me, frown lessening, a slightly sententious look coming over his face.) *A writer is someone who writes. Period. So stop wasting time and get to work. And leave me alone now—I've got to get this lousy thing finished.*

"OK. But Gog?"

What? I told you—

"Remember Lake McDonald?"

(Frowning much less all of a sudden, though still frowning a little, but with the slightest hint of an embarrassed smile concealed within the frown, and lips reflexively pursing in and out. How could I have forgotten this expression?) *Of course I do. Doc Beck's cabin on the lake. Good melon-cooling territory, as I recall.*

"Good steaks, too. Listen, Gog—"

What is it now?

"Could we maybe go on another camping trip sometime? With Zack?"

(His eyes suddenly grow shiny, and he blinks rapidly several times and swivels around in his chair so his back is to me when he speaks.) *I don't know. Maybe. We'll see. Leave me alone now.*

"OK, Gog. Goodbye."

(At the sound of this last word, suddenly wheeling back around to face me full on. His eyes are wet, and there is wetness on his cheeks, too. But his expression is fierce, almost frightening, as he admonishes me, one finger in the air.) *Never "Goodbye"—"So long."*

(Of course. I had almost forgotten that, too. Never "Goodbye," always "So long.")

"So long, Gog."

And shut the door on your way out, will you?

13

The Failure of Books

Diane used to say, "But Josh, it's not *in* a book." I would often come home with a bag of new books, which I would pretend to hide from her. I didn't want to hide them for real—what would have been the fun in that? Besides, really hiding them wasn't part of the game, which required that I only "try" to "hide" them, and that I then be "discovered," and my weakness "revealed."

It was a game that was not entirely a game—for her, because of financial anxiety; for me, because of guilt. Nevertheless, the ruse of the game provided some pleasure to offset the guilt and anxiety, as the day's haul of books was "reluctantly" produced and we went over it together.

My purchases would often baffle her: "Historiography? Since when did you get interested in historiography?" Or dismay her: "This Hitler thing is getting out of hand, Josh. When is it going to be over?" But sometimes they would please her: "'The Art of the Fillmore: The Poster Series, 1966–1971.' Oooh...." Art books pleased her most of all. She appreciated fine printing, calligraphy, and graphics. She herself made gorgeous greeting cards for family and friends, and wrote a beautiful hand. I didn't buy too many art books, though—not so much because they were too expensive, but because I enjoyed the feeling of specious practicality and fortitude I got by resisting a purchase that wasn't all that much of a temptation to begin with. For despite their weight, art books did not possess the sort of "heft" I was seeking.

By "heft" I mean something substantial, serious, intellectually nourishing, and—if possible—emotionally and spiritually nourishing as well. "Heft" is not predominantly a physical quality; though, all other things being equal, a physically heavy book is preferable to a light one. Factors such as a book's print, paper, page ornaments, and layout can all contribute to its "heft," but these are not primary. "Heft" is more a function of a book's "horizon of expectations" (see Chapter 9): that particular quality of hope and wishfulness engendered by the first encounter with a book, before its actual reading—a quality residing only in the mind of the book buyer, hopeful creature that he is. For obsessive book buying of the sort that possesses me is principally a thing of hope: hope misplaced, misguided, deluded even—but hope nonetheless.

I would enter the house quietly, books in bag. She would usually be sitting in the reclining chair in the living room, by the window (but not facing the window, so I could enter undetected). I would move rapidly, and with deliberate conspicuousness, down the narrow hallway (made narrower by deep bookshelves) that led past the living room into the kitchen, causing the bag to make as much noise as possible. (For this reason plastic was preferable; the point was only to *pretend* to be trying to get away with it.)

"All right, what did you get *this* time," she would sigh in exasperation, biting knowingly at the hook I had dangled in front of her. The game required me to play the part of the child caught with his hand in the cookie jar (or book bag). This too was deliberate. For if I was really only a child at heart, how could I be held fully responsible for my actions? On the other hand, if I was really a grown-up only playing the part of a child, out of guilt, how pathetic was that? Beneath the game, however, was the genuine financial anxiety that Diane felt up until the last month of her life, when my father died and left a substantial estate—too late for her to enjoy. We had always lived above our means, and it bothered her, and she worried.

A month after she died, at the start of the July 4 weekend, I walked out of Borders armed with five new books (full-price, too; more than a twinge of guilt there): three historiography books and two Hesse novels. I had already read Diane's copies of *The Glass Bead Game* (great heft—the hardbound edition of the 1969 Winstons' translation, with the Kandinsky-like dustcover: smooth paper, pleasing font, nifty page ornaments at the chapter breaks) and *Narcissus and Goldmund*, and was nearing the end of her copy of *Klingsor's Last Summer*. *Gertrude* and *Rosshalde* beckoned from the Borders' shelves, their odd foreign names evocative, bespeaking unplumbed mitteleuropean depth, complexity, intimacy, mystery that I had yet to be initiated into, and that added to their appeal. These were two that Diane didn't have. (As I would have rationalized to her later that evening, after having been "caught in the act.")

The phrase "armed with books" is not an idle metaphor. For me, books are a kind of protection, a defense—a weapon of the mind, to be used in virtuous battle. Battle against what? Against the enemies of mind, perhaps? (The phrase has a Trillingesque ring that appeals; Trilling, of course, has great "heft.") What do books help me feel protected against? Mindlessness? Brute force? Animal energies? In other words, against the world as it would be without books? The world as it really is? I don't know. I only know that I need to feel protected, and it helps to bring books with me into the empty bed. To have them around me when I go to sleep, and to see them on the night table when I wake up in the morning. Perhaps a killer who breaks into the house in the middle of the night will see that I am a virtuous reader, and spare me.

Notice that none of this has to do with the actual reading of books. The feelings that prompt me to buy books are external to the experience of reading. Indeed, many of the books I buy I will never read. I estimate that I have not read well over half the books that I own, and never will. Instead, I will buy more books. The emotions I experience—expectation, hope, desire, wishfulness—happen before I even begin reading a book, by virtue of not yet having begun it.

And the greatest of these is wishfulness. Mere wishfulness is the weakest, and vaguest, yet also most devout of the four emotions, and therefore comes closest to capturing my book-buying compulsion in all its reverent confusion. (Given that I really do not understand it myself. Which is why I am writing about it: I only write about things I don't understand.) The desire for knowledge; hope for the future—especially, the hope that once having gotten these newly purchased books under my mental belt, I will understand more, and better, than I do now (and so will not have to write about it); the expectation of some sort of reward, intellectual or spiritual, for having read (or at least bought) the books now in my possession—all these vague notions are in the air when I indulge my obsession. But wishfulness comes closest to conveying the elusive heart of my ardor, my need to be in possession of books—many of which I will never read. Of course I *hope* to read them, someday; and that wish seems more important than whether I actually do read them. Let the wish stand for the deed.

Books possessed and unread have more cachet than read books, but those unpossessed and unread have the most cachet of all, for they are still objects of the quest. They have not yet been deprived of the allure of wishfulness, or fallen victim to the inevitable disappointment of ownership. They have not yet become, in Mr. Sammler's phrase, "the wrong books." (All books, once possessed, become "the wrong books.")

But if I already know that the possession—not to mention the reading—of books is inevitably disappointing, then why do

I persist in buying them? For one, because my wishfulness is stronger than my knowledge. I know that once I own a book, its possession will immediately disappoint me; but I can't resist the wish to own it. Couldn't I have been satisfied by taking it out of the library? (I hear Diane's voice again here; her exasperated question is not without an indulgent warmth.) Not only have I not been satisfied, but immediately after buying it I feel a familiar, guilty frustration: This is not the right book, either.

It would be hard to say which is stronger, the frustration or the guilt. But they really cannot be separated, like the feeling I used to get as a boy when I ran hot water over the poison oak lesions on my hands and arms. Was it pain or a delectable, almost unbearable pleasure that I felt? I didn't know; all I knew was that I couldn't turn the faucet off until my lesions were bright red and throbbing. Just as I cannot now refrain from the next book purchase until it is in the bag, at which point it becomes no longer a comfort but an indictment, like the inflamed rash on my hands.

Another aspect of my book-buying compulsion, besides defense and temptation, is the need to be filled by the kinds of nourishment that books have to offer. This is not to be confused with the more abstract (and in my case less insatiable) desire for knowledge. The need to be filled, while greater now than ever, is not new. It was there long before I met Diane. In college, I would haunt the bookstores on Telegraph Avenue: Cody's, Moe's, Shakespeare's. And after college, in New York: New Yorker Books, Coliseum Books, the Gotham Book Mart ("Wise Men Fish Here"), Argosy Books—they all felt my hunger, the insatiable hunger of my lonely need. I have no doubt there was a sexual element in my bibliophagy. The possession of books as a substitute—a poor, cold substitute, but it had its small pleasures—for the possession of a woman. There will be nothing again, thank God, like the lonely book buying of my youth. Though I wonder: will the book buying of my widowed middle age be any better? To judge from the way it's going so far, no.

The painful, fleeting intensities of youth, which tend to make most things feel worse than they are, will be replaced by the gradual incapacitations of age, still guided by younger impulses, yet without being able to satisfy them.

After I moved in with Diane, the book buying continued. At first, we bought books together; but she soon got a sense of who she was dealing with, and gradually changed her role from accomplice, to sympathetic confidante, to dubious observer—and then, when all else failed, to exasperated remonstrator. Nor was she deceived when my purchases were masked as gifts to her; for these "gifts" had a way of migrating over to my side of the bed. When I snuggled up with a book I had ostensibly bought for her, the knowledge of my bad faith cast a little pall over its enjoyment.

Reading in bed was something we loved doing together. Looking back on it, I really think we loved doing it as much as anything else in bed. In some ways it was an extension of our sex life—a confirmation, if not consummation, of our intimacy. We used to joke that we had always been looking for someone to read in bed with. It was yet another sign of "coming home."

But reading in bed with her did not satisfy my passion for acquiring more books. It may even have inflamed it, in some ways. After all, now my book buying had yet another motive: I could look forward to coming home and falling into bed that night, book in hand, next to my love, who was similarly equipped. The desire for more books and the desire for more sex are perhaps analogous in their greed: placation of the immediate desire does not produce satisfaction—only more desire.

A therapist once asked me, when I was in my 20s, "Do you want to be old?" The answer I gave her then, unhesitatingly, was "Yes." And that would still be my answer (granted that now, in middle age, I'm a lot closer to that goal). Not because I really want to be old, but because I want to be wise. And wisdom is usually seen as a product of age (and books, of course). As though, if one lives long enough, and reads enough books, one will acquire wisdom. One will have reached a raised, secure vantage point—an upstairs library, say, with the sun streaming in through the windows—from which one can look down upon the landscape of one's life below, lying there softly illumined by the antique light of age, and "contemplate about" it with the assured hindsight of wisdom. Perhaps it is this desire, too—the desire for a secure vantage point of wisdom—that fuels my book buying. As if the "right book," were I finally to discover it, could somehow tie up the loose ends of my life and show me the way to the book-lined room, with the afternoon sunlight streaming in through the windows.

But I know I'm never going to get there. And what's more, I don't even really *want* to get there. The sun-filled, book-lined room beckons temptingly, but remains out of reach. It reminds me of my childhood "View-Finder." When I was a very young child—three or four or five—I remember wanting to live in the amazingly three-dimensional scenes from *Alice in Wonderland* and *Br'er Rabbit* that had somehow gotten themselves contained in the circular slides that I could insert into the top slot of my brown plastic stereoscopic "View-Finder." I remember how hard it was for me to accept that I couldn't actually enter into and inhabit those astonishing little worlds, which beckoned so temptingly from inside the device. It is almost as hard for me, now, to leave behind the vision of the book-lined room in the afternoon sunlight. But leave it I must, because—like the scenes inside the View-Finder—there is no life there, only a tantalizing, wished-for illusion.

"Life," Milan Kundera wrote in the title to a novel, "Is Elsewhere." Diane gave me that book. Largely, I think, because of one of the chapter titles: "The Poet Masturbates." But we're not going there. We're going elsewhere, beyond the book-lined room. Life is out there, in the sun—in the direct, unfiltered, un-antique sunlight. While the book-lined room, like the world inside the "View-Finder," continues to exert its attractions, I know there is no real nourishment in it. And there is no ultimate nourishment in books, either. (Which is why I keep buying and buying them, and am never satisfied.) Not in their reading, nor in their possession. There is nourishment only in the life that books come from. In the struggle, not the settling. In the changing, not the fixed. In the present-day light, not the antique one.

But Josh, it's not in *a book.* I know that now. Or rather, I am coming to know it. The hard way. Without you, Dee. I am a slow learner. You will be patient with me, won't you? After all, now you have all the time in the world. But I don't. Which is why I must leave the book-lined room, and find a scene of writing in the sun. Only when we come to experience the failure of books can we begin to write. Write about what? About failure, of course. What other subject is there for me? You might even say it's the story of my life.